"Quick, where's my goggles?! Halfway through these wonderful athlete profiles, I could stand it no more—I simply had to find the nearest pool and go for a swim! Each story is a motivator. Each voice reminds us why we love this tough, honest sport of ours. If you take swimming seriously, you're going to connect with these pages."

—P.H. Mullen, author of *Gold in the Water*

"If you've ever wondered 'What is it about swimming that makes champions go through all that work and pain?' this book will provide the answer. I've been privileged to know many of the swimmers profiled herein, and I can honestly say, their stories are worth reading. Larry Thompson has assembled a fine collection of swimmers to profile in his book, *Swimmers: Courage and Triumph* and every swimming fan and reader will benefit from knowing their stories."

—John Naber, Olympic swimming champion, television announcer, author and motivational speaker

"*Swimmers: Courage and Triumph* captures the essence of what happens when the human spirit uses the element of water to overcome challenges, both mentally and physically, in order to break through boundaries set by the mind or body.

This is a must read for anyone who is passionate about swimming. More importantly, this is a must read for anyone who needs inspiration to reach a life goal. The book inspires all readers to realize that all triumph originates with courage.

The book does a fantastic job of detailing how each triumph has its place in history, beginning with Mark Spitz's seven world records in the 1972 Olympic Games all the way to Lynne Cox's historical swim to Antarctica. Readers will enjoy learning about such people as Rich Abrahams who broke age barriers with his world record swims. Other stories such as the lives of David Yudovin who survived cardiac arrest and George Brunstad at age 70 who both went on to swim the English Channel are equally inspirational. Every reader will enjoy the stories shared in *Swimmers: Courage and Triumph*. I know I did!"

—Brent Rutemiller, Publisher of *Swimming World Magazine*

"Larry gives us a brief glimpse into the lives and accomplishments of truly extraordinary individuals who through their passion and commitment have achieved greatness in the aquatic community. And while these people come from all walks of life, having unique goals and experiences, Larry's depiction of their enthusiasm for swimming and their courage is an inspiration to all members of our aquatic family and to the public at large."

—Rob Copeland, President - United States Masters Swimming

Swimmers: Courage and Triumph

Edited and Photographed by Larry Thompson.
Written Profiles by John Lohn, Kari Lydersen, Jeremy Shweder,
Bill Volckening and Phil Whitten.

ISHOF Publishing

ISBN-13: 978-1-887359-02-3
ISBN-10: 1-887359-02-8
Printed in Canada

ISHOF Publishing
One Hall of Fame Drive
Fort Lauderdale, Florida 33316
p (954)462-6536 / f (954)525-4031
www.ishof.org

First Edition

Cover Design by Gabriele Wilson

In memory of my Dad

Acknowledgments

I would like to thank our writers Phil Whitten, Kari Lydersen, John Lohn, Bill Volckening and Jeremy Shweder for the enthusiasm, dedication and insight they've brought to this project. Many others have made significant contributions including those who have assisted in finding and engaging our swimmers; Tracy Grilli, Barbara Hummel, Janel Jorgensen, Lee Lawrence, Janey Miller, Heather Novickis, Evan Morgenstein, Laura Cutler, John Naber and Bill Roberts; my very patient assistants Barbara McCormack, and Michaela Gordon; Jim Dickson who pilots a sure and steady boat; and those helping to make this book a reality, Martha Kaplan, Nancy Nicholas, Peter Spectre, Laurie Marchwinski, Gay DeMario, Michael Gero; our excellent cover designer and collaborator Gabriele Wilson; and especially Tom Lachocki and Bruce Wigo who helped to make this book possible.

Most of all I would like to thank our swimmers who have inspired us all to live with more courage and to help us overcome the obstacles that sometimes get in the way of achieving our personal triumphs.

Larry Thompson
April, 2007

Healthy Pools. Healthy Bodies.

The National Swimming Pool Foundation® (NSPF®) is proud to sponsor this wonderful collection of 19 stories that portray outstanding aquatic role models. In our mission to encourage healthier living through aquatic education and research, we believe these motivating stories will inspire many to healthier and more positive lives. We are thankful for organizations like the ISHOF who help further the awareness and appreciation of aquatic health benefits.

It remains important to fund research, to present science-based education, and to disseminate knowledge via conferences and scholarly journals. Research and education impact our society, and we are committed to their advance. The stories told here impact us with the most powerful force - passion. The eyes, hearts, and actions of our brothers and sisters are a beacon we wish to reflect. Though our light may not be as bright, their passion wraps around us like strong arms. Their stories influence and guide our stories to a brighter future.

Water will continue to play a pivotal role to prevent pain and propel us away from the maladies caused by sedentary living. We hope you find this book an inspiration, and share it with many.

With admiration,

Thomas M. Lachocki, Ph.D.
CEO
National Swimming Pool Foundation

Profiles Were Contributed by

John Lohn contributed written profiles for
Martiza Correia and Mike Nyeholt.

Kari Lydersen contributed written profiles for
Melanie Benn, Jeff Keith, Rowdy Gaines,
Marcella MacDonald D.P.M. and Noah White.

Jeremy Shweder contributed written profiles for
Dawn Blue Gerken, Chris Swain,
Jenny Thompson and David Yudovin.

Bill Volckening contributed written profiles for
George Brunstad, Natalie Coughlin
and Terry Laughlin.

Phil Whitten contributed written profiles for
Rich Abrahams, Greg Bonnan, Lynne Cox,
Dave Denniston and Mark Spitz.

Swimmers

swimmers

COURAGE & TRIUMPH

LARRY THOMPSON

Mark Spitz

It has been 35 years since Mark Spitz delivered what is widely acknowledged as the greatest performance in Olympic history. Not Olympic swimming history. Olympic history.

For the 11 readers who may not be sure of what he did, here it is in a nutshell: 7 events, 7 gold medals, 7 world records. The 100 free, 200 free, 100 fly, 200 fly, 400 free relay, 800 free relay, 400 medley relay: gold, gold, gold, gold, gold, gold, gold. World records every time.

When Michael Phelps was challenging Spitz's seven golds at the Athens Olympics in 2004, he entered eight events. He wound up with six golds – only one fewer than Spitz – and two bronze. And in all the media frenzy surrounding Phelps' challenge, no one even mentioned Spitz's seven world records. As great an athlete as Michael is, no one thought that he'd set a world record in every final. (Actually, he set one, in the 400 IM).

Thirty five years have passed since Spitz's incredible performance in Munich, and there have been some extraordinary swimmers who have swum and strutted on the world stage. Janet Evans, Summer Sanders, Kristina Egerszegi, Jenny Thompson, Natalie Coughlin, Katie Hoff, John Naber, Rowdy Gaines, Matt Biondi, Alex Popov, Gary Hall, Ian Thorpe, Grant Hackett, Pieter van den Hoogenband and, recently, Michael Phelps have all had their turns. Great swimmers all. Magnificent athletes, every one. But as far as the general public is concerned, Mark Spitz is the swimmer they know and admire most. For many, Mark Spitz is still the only swimmer they know.

Part of the reason Spitz is so memorable is that famous poster of him, draped with his seven Olympic gold medals, and wearing nothing but a Speedo, a mustache and a warm smile. The poster, which sold over five million copies, etched a triumphant 22 year old Mark Spitz forever in our memories.

Today, at 57, Spitz is no longer the Golden Boy. The mustache is gone, the black hair has turned a dignified gray, and about 20 pounds have been added to his once lean, sculpted body. But he has aged well and the smile, now framed by laugh lines, makes him instantly recognizable.

In the public consciousness, Mark Spitz remains the consummate competitor. He is that, of course, but there is – and always was – a deeper side to him. For one thing, he is a master of psyching out potential challengers. "At the highest level, every sport is 90 percent mental," he believes. "Everyone is talented, everyone has good technique, everyone has worked hard. So you've got to find something that will give you that tiny advantage. For me, that is and always has been the psychological side of the game. I was always trying to gain a psychological advantage, to inculcate in the minds of my toughest competitors that they couldn't beat me."

Swimming at Santa Clara Swim Club, Spitz trained daily with some of the greatest swimmers in the world including his hero, Don Schollander, and Dick Roth. He trained hard, but he never became a super-trainer, as did his Indiana University teammates John Kinsella, Charlie Hickox and Gary Hall – world record holders all, and all able to crank out incredible workout times, day after day. That was part of his strategy, to send these guys he admired enormously an unmistakable message, "You will never beat me." He relied on (1) mastering the "get out" swim and (2) holding back just enough during a set to be able to swim an amazing final repeat.

The "get out" swim was called every now and then, by the IU coach, Doc Counsilman. At some point past the middle of a planned workout, Doc would select one swimmer to swim an event, starting from the blocks. A time, very near the swimmer's lifetime best – which in the case of the IU team often meant near the American or world record – was set as a goal. If the swimmer beat the goal time, everyone could get out. The workout would be over. If he missed it, everyone climbed back in the pool and the workout resumed.

Doc often chose Mark. At that time, Spitz's American record in the 100 yard fly stood at 49.1 seconds. Doc would say, "Okay. If Mark can go under 50 seconds, you guys can all get out."

Talk about pressure! With his teammates cheering him on, Mark would zoom up the pool, then back, then up and back again. More often than not, Doc would announce "49.7" or "49.6." Mark was the hero for the day, as everyone ran for the showers.

From Spitz's point of view, he was sending a silent message. "This guy can swim close to record times during practice, unshaved and unrested. Imagine what he could do at a meet when he's shaved and rested!"

As for his second strategy, Mark Wallace, the IU team manager and to this day one of Spitz's closest friends recalls, "Let's say they were doing a set of ten 200's free. Mark, who held the American record then in the 200 free at 1:39.5, would get in a lane next to Gary Hall and stay at his hips for the first nine repeats. Gary might go 1:48, while Mark would be 1:49 or 1:50. On the last one, everyone would go all out. Gary would get down to a 1:46 or so – a great time – but Mark, who had rationed his energy for the first nine swims, would blow everyone away, and go, say, a 1:41, leaving Gary and everyone else, in his wake.

"Gary should have been pleased. His cumulative time was several seconds better than Mark's. But all he could think of was Mark's ability to swim a 1:41 at the end of a tough set!"

Mission accomplished.

While Spitz was a master at the mental game, he wasn't the only such master on the IU deck. Wallace recalls the 1971 NCAA's, where Doc kept Mark from psyching himself out.

"The meet was at Iowa State and we had just arrived. Mark didn't look very well. He came up to Doc and said, 'I'm kinda itching and it looks like I have some kind of a rash.'"

"Doc, who had raised four kids with his wife, Marge, took one look at the blotchy red marks, and knew Mark had the measles. Now Mark was tough as nails, but he was also very sensitive. Doc knew that if Mark knew he had the measles, he'd psyche himself out. So Doc said, 'You're right. It is a rash. You probably got that when you shaved down last night. Don't worry about it. It'll go away.' He then enlisted me, Mark's roommates, and a few other guys to help with the deception."

"The next day, which was the first day of the NCAA's, Mark was feeling worse. He had a fever and the measles had spread. 'Don't worry,' Doc assured him, 'it's just a rash.' His teammates agreed."

"So Mark swam the entire three days of the meet with the measles and a fever, and he won two events."

Spitz counts "The Great Mustache Caper" as his greatest psychological triumph. It took place at the 1972 Olympics in Munich.

Back then, none of the men wore caps, and goggles were still not permitted. Swimmers had been shaving their bodies since 1956, and in Munich, some even shaved their heads.

Not Spitz. He showed up with a full mop of hair and a mustache. During the week before the Games began, teams often overlapped at training sessions.

Spitz recalls with glee what happened next. "One day, the Russian coach came up to me and asked if I planned to shave my mustache when the competition began. 'It just adds resistance when you're swimming,' he informed me, quite correctly."

"'No way,' I told him. 'We did some studies on water flow with and without the mustache. We discovered was that the mustache helps channel the water behind me and actually makes me more streamlined. It makes me faster!' I could barely keep myself from laughing, but he took me quite seriously."

"The next year, at the World Championships, half the men on the Russian team sported mustaches," he laughs.

After Munich, on the advice of his agent at the William Morris Agency, Spitz postponed going to dental school at USC to launch an acting career. After all, he was incredibly popular and very good looking. What more could anyone ask?

Well, acting skills for one. He had none. Super-humanly graceful in the water, he was stiff as a board on the stage. Had the agency arranged for him to take acting lessons, he might have been successful as an actor, but he was thrown, totally unprepared, into the lions' den. And was gobbled up.

Spitz never went to dental school, something he regrets to this day. He laughs though, noting "I still get five to ten letters a week addressed to 'Dr. Mark Spitz.' I may be the most famous dentist who's not a dentist in the world."

Though never a dentist, Spitz has built a successful post Olympics career for himself as a real estate developer, financial adviser, corporate spokesperson and motivational speaker. He's constantly on the go, with speaking engagements taking him to every corner of the United States and around the world, from Brazil to Qatar. He is happily married to his college sweetheart, Susie, and they have two sons, Matthew and Justin. Neither boy is a competitive swimmer though both are good athletes.

Mark Spitz has also mellowed over the years, the sharper edges of his personality having become smoother. Today he is personable, creative, confident, intelligent and witty. He also acknowledges his obligation to give back to the sport that has given him so much. That's why, when he was offered the position of Chairman of the Board of the International Swimming Hall of Fame (ISHOF) by Executive Director Bruce Wigo in 2005, he accepted without hesitation.

For Spitz though, taking it on is a calling. "So much has taken place in our sport over the last 150 years, some of it amazing, some of it incredibly amusing. There have been so many great characters whose stories should be more widely known. It's all part of our legacy. Using 21st century interactive technology, it's our responsibility to communicate that history to current generations and pass it along to future ones."

Mark was photographed December 11, 2006 on Manhattan Beach, California.
Profile contributed by Phil Whitten.

Lynne Cox

SHE can't break a minute for 100 meters freestyle, and never could. She's a distance swimmer but she's never even come close to cracking 9 minutes for 800 meters. Though she's trained and roomed with some of history's most storied Olympians, she never made the U.S. Olympic team, and never will.

Still, Lynne Cox is one of the most remarkable swimmers ever. Companion to a plethora of aquatic citizens – from plankton to penguins and jelly fish to whales – she has ventured where no human had gone before. Along the way, her aquatic accomplishments have been responsible for cleaning up a polluted river, advancing scientific knowledge about human physiological limits and even bringing about the signing of a nuclear test ban treaty between the United States and the former Soviet Union.

Lynne's remarkable journey began conventionally enough in New England. At the age of three in Maine, she was taught to swim by her grandfather in Snow Pond – the same place he'd taught her mother to swim. By the time Lynne was seven, she was competing in local meets in New Hampshire.

Her parents, who sensed their children had untapped swimming talent, moved the family, Lynne, sisters Laura and Ruth, and brother David in 1969 to the nation's swimming mecca, southern California. There she trained at the Phillips 66 Swim Club in Long Beach under the watchful eye of U.S. Olympic coach Don Gambril. Back then, Gambril had the top men's team in the U.S., as well as one of the strongest women's teams. So Lynne found herself in the water with Olympic greats, including Gunnar Larsson of Sweden, Hans Fassnacht of Germany, Bruce and Steve Furniss, Shirley Babashoff and Gary Hall – the best all-around swimmer in the world at that time.

It was inspiring company and, Gambril recalls, "Lynne went all out in every set in every workout. But," he concluded, "she just didn't have enough fast-twitch muscle fibers."

"She had a great attitude, always cheerful and smiling. She worked as hard as any of the swimmers in the pool. But she just didn't have the speed. It was clear, she would never be a top competitive swimmer."

"On the other hand," Gambril recounts, "even at 12 she could swim forever – and hold a pretty fast pace. What's more, cold water, or what we thought of as cold water back then, didn't seem to bother her at all."

Gambril learned that a friend of his, Ron Blackledge, was training a group of young teens to swim the Catalina Channel, a 27 mile jaunt from Santa Catalina Island to the mainland. He urged Lynne to join the group and she did.

In August, 1971, at the age of 14, Lynne and three of her teammates completed the swim, with Lynne finishing in 12 hours, 36 minutes. "As I touched the shore, I knew that I wanted to swim the English Channel, the Mt. Everest of distance swimming.'

The water in the English Channel in summer is between 55 and 60 degrees fahrenheit – some 5 to 10 degrees colder than the Catalina Channel in August. Wetsuits, however, are verboten. Under the rules established by the English Channel Swimming Association, swimmers may wear only a "standard swimming costume," swim suit, cap and goggles. A layer of grease is permitted.

The cold water has been a source of frustration for hundreds of would-be Channel conquerors. Many have been forced to quit short of their goal. Some have gone into hypothermia and several have died. Lynne felt she could handle the distance, which is 21 miles as the dolphin swims, but can range to up to 30 miles or more depending on the currents. She had no idea whether she could survive the cold water.

Fortunately, she had a secret weapon, her dad. "My father, who is a physician, believed that the more I could acclimate to cold water during the year, the less stressful my swim would be. I began swimming only in the Pacific Ocean, and I continued during the winter, when the water temperature dropped as low as 50 degrees. I wore light clothes all year long and always slept without blankets and with the windows open.

Her father was right. At fifteen, and less than one year after her Catalina swim, she not only broke the women's record for the Channel swim with a time of nine hours 57 minutes, she broke the men's record as well.

Her record for the overall fastest time lasted just three weeks, when American Richard Hart clocked 9 hours 44 minutes. Undaunted, Lynne returned the following year and then the 16 year old took the mark down to 9:36.

So what do you do when you're 16 and you've accomplished what most folks regard as the ultimate in the sport of open water swimming?

Why, you reach beyond the ultimate, of course. "I wanted to do something that had never been done before," Lynne explains. No more repeating what others have already done. After all, there have to be firsts – Matthew Webb conquering the Channel back in 1875 and Sir Edmund Hillary successfully ascending Mt. Everest in 1953.

So Lynne set her sights on the Cook Strait, a treacherous bit of ocean separating New

Zealand's North and South Islands.

Three men had crossed the forbidding, turbulent, shark-infested, 10 mile strait, but no woman had ever made it. "I figured I could make the crossing in about four hours," Lynne recalls.

Ah, the hubris of youth! On a warm mid summer day in February of 1975, Lynn entered the 50 degree water and began stroking. Five hours later, she was farther from the finish than when she started.

"We didn't have the scientific equipment we have today – detailed tidal forecasts, up-to-the second weather and ocean reports from a network of satellites. You just got in and swam."

"Shortly after I got in, the winds were gusting up to 40 knots. Combined with the nasty 9 foot waves, I was being tossed around like flotsam, and I began to question whether I could continue. But the crew in my support boat included a radio announcer who was broadcasting news about the swim. Listeners began calling in, and the announcer relayed their words to me."

"Somehow, their support gave me renewed strength and after a harrowing 12 hours, and accompanied the last half hour or so by some 50 to 60 playful dolphins, I crawled up on the beach on South Island. The next day, church bells rang throughout the country to celebrate the swim. I felt as though New Zealanders had shared my struggle. That made me realizes that a swim could be more than just an athletic event. It could be a way of bringing people together, perhaps even of opening borders."

That realization was to shape the challenges Lynne took on for the next three decades.

In 1976 she crossed the Strait of Magellan, a watery graveyard for ships off the southern coast of Chile. The following years saw her swim around the Cape of Good Hope, at the southern tip of South Africa, where she narrowly escaped a shark attack; across Lake Titicaca, from Bolivia to Peru; and through the Gulf of Aqaba, from Egypt to Israel and then from Israel to Jordan.

It was in 1987, when Lynne was 30 years old, that she completed an amazing swim that united two continents, reunited long-separated families and ultimately affected world politics.

On August 8, Lynne completed a 5 mile swim in the frigid waters of the Bering Sea, stroking from Little Diomede Island in Alaska, cross the International Date Line, to Big Diomede Island in Siberia. She had waited 11 long years for permission from Soviet authorities, and few experts thought she could last for more than a few yards in the icy, 38 degree water. But despite a thick fog that sent her off course, she never faltered. Two hours six minutes after setting out from Alaska, she had swum to the USSR.

Upon her arrival, she was greeted by Soviet officials, scientists and athletes, then taken to a tent, where Russian doctors warmed her up as the local Inuit feasted in honor of her accomplishment. In the spirit of the moment, Soviet authorities relaxed a 48 year embargo on travel and family members from the two islands, only seventh-tenths of a mile apart, were joyously reunited.

Four months later, U.S. President Ronald Reagan and Russian President Mikhail Gorbachev met at the White House to sign the INF Missile Treaty. During the ceremony, President Gorbachev offered a toast, saying, "Last summer it took one brave American by the name of Lynne Cox just two hours to swim from one of our countries to the other. We saw on television how sincere and friendly the meeting was between our people and the Americans when she stepped onto the Soviet shore. She proved by her courage how close to each other our peoples live."

"I was thrilled," Lynne recalls exuberantly. "Having President Gorbachev acknowledge the swim at the White House during the historic signing of the INF Missile Treaty was beyond anything I could have ever imagined. It told me that he completely understood my reason for the swim and that he held the same belief that we could become friends. More than that, the treaty signing between President Reagan and President Gorbachev demonstrated that belief. Sometimes you have dreams, sometimes they are big, but you can never imagine how far they will go, or how they might inspire someone to do something more."

Nowadays, Lynne Cox is best known for her most recent impossible feat, swimming more than a mile in the 32 degree waters of Antarctica.

The swim, in 2003, which represented the fulfillment of a lifelong dream, was faithfully chronicled by ABC's "60 Minutes." It is also almost lyrically described by Lynne, herself, in her best selling book "Swimming to Antarctica".

The swim, which probably would quickly have killed any other human being on this blue planet, was not undertaken as a spur-of-the moment decision. Lynne planned every detail meticulously, enlisting the assistance of Dr Bill Keatinge of the University of London, a pioneer in the study of hypothermia, and keeping safety foremost in her mind. No one before her was known to have survived more than a very short time – five minutes at most – in 32 degree water. There were no guarantees that she would be able to last much longer.

"We were able to confirm that she can maintain stable body temperature with her head out of the water in water temperatures as low as 44 degrees Fahrenheit," he told "60 Minutes" correspondent, Scott Pelley. "We've got one other person that we know can do that. He was an Icelander who swam ashore from an overturned boat."

Keatinge explained that anyone else would immediately feel the pain as if from an electric shock – their muscles would flail and their heart would stop in minutes. "In technical terms, your heart would go into ventricular fibrillation. Then, you're dead."

Keatinge believes that Cox has trained her body to keep most of her blood at her body's core and away from the skin where it's exposed to the cold. She also has an even layer of fat to insulate her body from the cold.

Lynne concurs. "If you look at the marine mammals in Antarctica, the whales, the walruses, the seals all have body fat to stay warm. Their blubber is very dense whereas mine will be more like a cotton sweater. But I'm not going to be in as long as they are."

But Lynne wasn't relying solely on her "cotton sweater" layer of fat to bring her in safely. She trained harder than ever before, lifting weights to increase her upper body strength because she planned to swim with her head out of water, focusing on rapid-turnover sprinting. She also returned to swimming only in the cold Pacific near her Los Alamitos, California home and taking only cold baths and showers.

All these preparations paid off. Despite her fear of icebergs, not to mention orcas or leopard seals mistaking her for a seal, Lynne swam a total of 1.22 miles in the ice cold water. It took her exactly 25 minutes, escorted the final 100 meters by an exuberant pod of penguins.

That's an average of just over 19 minutes per 1500 meters – a remarkably fast pace. What's more, she did it with her head out of water, water polo style, with no turns. And at the age of 46!

"I guarantee you," said her old coach, Don Gambril, "that's faster than she ever swam in a pool."

So what's next for this smiling barrier-buster, this ever cheerful pioneer? She seems to have done it all. Perhaps she can try a four lap individual medley across the Cook Strait, one crossing using each stroke, a writer suggests.

"No, I probably won't do that," she says. "Actually, I don't know what my next challenge will be."

Whatever it turns out to be, we can be sure it will further our understanding of what is humanly possible, and it will serve to bring people together.

Lynn was photographed February 24, 2005 on the banks of the Charles River in Boston, Massachusetts.

Profile contributed by Phil Whitten.

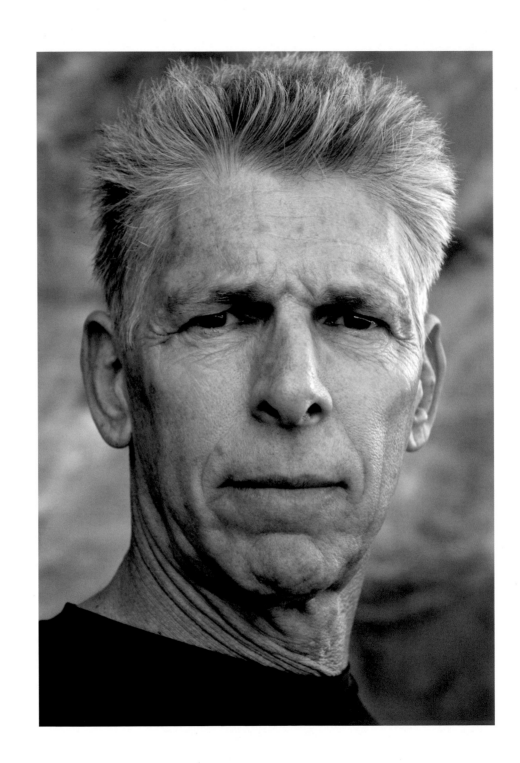

Rich Abrahams

A pioneer, Richard Abrahams is one of a handful of men and women venturing into an uncharted wilderness and hacking a path for the rest of us to follow. Through his achievements which are every bit as significant as Roger Bannister breaking the 4 minute barrier for the mile run, if accompanied by less fanfare, Abrahams is doing nothing less than redefining what is physically possible as we reach 40, 50, 60 and beyond.

Until the 1970's, the rule of thumb in gerontology was that our physical and physiological capabilities declined at the rate of about one percent per year, beginning at age 25 until we reached 60. After that, the rate of decline increased every year. It was a dismal picture.

Since then, largely thanks to studies of Masters athletes, most notably swimmers, we've learned that much of the decline previously thought to be "natural," was actually a consequence of our unnatural, sedentary lifestyles. People who exercise regularly do not begin to decline until their early thirties, with the rate of decline a tiny fraction of one percent. In fact, Masters swimmers do not experience a one percent per year decline until their early seventies. What this means is that a 70 year old Masters swimmer who trains moderately on a regular basis is, physically, the equivalent of a "normal" 45 year old.

But Abrahams has demonstrated that even this is by no means the final word on the subject. At age 60, he is essentially as fast as he was at 55, 50, 45, 40... and 20, when he finished second at the NCAA Swimming Championships.

Today, at 61, Abrahams stands 6 feet 2 inches tall, the same as when he was a collegiate swimmer for Northwestern University in the mid 1960's. He's still a trim 170 pounds. His chest and waist measurements – 42 and 32 inches, respectively – are also the same, as is his 45 beats-per-minute resting pulse.

"Well," you might say, "he's probably trained hard all his life, never taking the time to smell the roses, toss back a few cool ones or smoke a cigarette."

You'd be wrong.

Abrahams, born in Brooklyn, spent his childhood in Scarsdale, New York far from the swimming meccas of northern and southern California and Florida. His family belonged to a beach and tennis club, but young Richard did most of his swimming in Long Island Sound.

Every July 4th and Labor Day, the club would have a cookout and put on a children's swim meet, with the races set at 25 yards for the younger kids and 50 yards for the older ones. Rich was good but by no means a world-beater. "Every year, from the time I was eight until I was 12, I'd finish second to the same kid."

Then, just before his 14th birthday, the Abrahams family moved to North Miami Beach, Florida where Rich attended North Miami High. He went out for swimming his freshman year and made the team, but he was no ball of fire.

"Actually, I made the 'B' team," he recalls. "The faster kids, who swam year around, were on the 'A' team. The B team got to swim against the weaker teams in our league, but since I was one of the slowest kids on the B team, I didn't compete much that year."

That summer, Rich swam for a local AAU team and dropped his time to 25.5 for the 50 yard freestyle. "The high school coach was at that meet and I was thrilled when he congratulated me," he says.

Abrahams kept on improving. By his junior year he was third in the state in the 100 fly. In 1962, his senior year, he won All City honors with a 23.2 for the 50 free and 57.5 for the 100 fly. When Northwestern University offered him a half scholarship, he jumped at the opportunity.

While Abrahams had become a pretty good 100 yard flyer, no one had told him that the distance in college dual meets back then was 200 yards. "I must've been in shock," he says, "because I have absolutely no memories of my freshman year."

Still, Rich must have gone to work because by his sophomore year he was a pretty fair 200 flyer. Unfortunately, there were several seniors who were faster, so he never got to swim it. Nor did he swim the 100 fly on the medley relay. Apparently, however, as little more than an afterthought, the coach entered him in the 50 and 100 free at the Big 10 Championships that year. To the surprise of everyone – and no one more than Rich, himself – he uncorked a 21.6 in the prelims of the 50, tying the pool record held by American record holder Steve Jackman. Abrahams went on to win the final in 21.9 and placed fourth in the 100 with a 49.1.

Those performances took him to the 1964 NCAA Championships, the first Wildcat swimmer to compete at that meet in nearly a decade. Abrahams finished fifth in the 50 (21.9) and qualified for the U.S. Olympic Trials in the 100.

"I was very happy to make the Olympic Trials, but you've got to remember that back then it wasn't the big thing it is now," he recalls. "Our family moved to Savannah, Georgia that spring, and after the NCAA's, I didn't even get into the water until mid June. That's when I joined a small, local team and began training."

The Trials were in Astoria, New York in the borough of Queens, that summer and Rich drove up with his mother. "I slept on the couch at my grandmother's house, and my mother didn't come to watch me swim which," he adds, "was okay. She preferred to go shopping," he says.

With no experience swimming long course, Rich didn't make the finals but was thrilled to watch such greats as Don Schollander, Steve Clark and Dick Roth.

By his own reckoning, Rich "got serious" the next year, placing second at the NCAA's in the 50 free and just missing the finals in the 100. In the summer of '65, he trained long course for the first time and made the U.S. Maccabiah Games team. In the 100 meter final in Israel, he went out too fast (24.8), then barely held off a fast closing field to win in 56.2.

At the Big 10 championships in his senior year Abrahams won the 50 free and finally won the 100, clocking 47.6. He also pushed himself beyond his limits, swimming an amazing 46.0 while anchoring the Wildcat freestyle relay, an effort that left him lying on the pool deck unable to walk for an hour.

Then his swimming career was over. Or so he thought.

No more fun and games. It was time to get serious about life. So Abrahams moved back to the Big Apple, enrolled in Columbia Law School and took a job as personal assistant for the Rockefeller family.

The next few years saw a lot of changes. He took a job at the New York law firm of Chadbourne & Parke, got married, dropped out to backpack around Europe for six months, bought a VW bus, and moved to Denver. "The world was very exciting in those days," Rich says. "I have no regrets."

Still searching for his place in the world, he opened a law practice in Denver with a former college roommate. "It was the antithesis of Chadbourne & Parke," he muses. "There we were very selective about our clients – only major international corporations and the very rich. In Denver, all they had to do was walk through the doorway."

"I hated it," recalls Rich. What he enjoyed was playing sports, basketball, football and baseball, on weekends. So he simply walked away from his practice and enrolled in an MA program in Recreation at the University of Colorado, a change that did not sit all that well with his wife.

At Colorado, exercise physiology became his passion. Meanwhile, having suffered recurrent injuries playing basketball, he decided to get back in the pool. He had become a two-packs-a-day Marlboro Man, and the first time was sobering. "I had planned to warm-up with an easy 400 yards, but I couldn't make it. I had to stop and rest after 200 yards."

In February of 1974, just shy of his 30th birthday and still sporting a full beard and earring, he entered his first Masters meet and swam 22.9 for the 50 free. "That floored me," he laughs. "Everyone was so nice, so accepting and encouraging, I decided to stick with the swimming."

It was two years before he swam at a Masters Nationals, where he picked up a silver medal in the 50. More importantly, while working at the Human Performance Lab in Boulder, he gradually constructed a training regimen that, he felt would pay off both in

performance and in maintaining lifetime fitness. By then, the beard, earring and cigarettes were gone.

In 1980, Abrahams hooked up with Bill Abbott, who became his regular training partner and remains so. It was Abbott who convinced him to swim seriously. Today, the two men swim four to five times a week and devote two workouts per week to dryland training, alternating between intense and "easy" workouts.

"My workouts don't mimic the motions of the four swimming strokes," Abrahams explains. "I just focus on becoming generally strong, with special emphasis on the core and legs." The training reaches a peak about two weeks before a major meet. Then he tapers for two weeks, sharpening his sprinting skills while resting to regain his strength.

That's when Rich Abrahams is ready to rumble.

"It's all in the preparation," he intones. "The will to win is nothing without the will to prepare."

At 40, Rich set his first national record, swimming 22.22 for the 50 free at the 1984 USMS Nationals in Brown Deer, Wisconsin. It was six more years before he swam in his first long course meet, but when he did his debut was sensational. Competing at the World Championships in Rio de Janeiro, he rocketed through the 50 meter free in 25.30, a world record for men 45-49.

The next few years were rough – his marriage broke up and it took him three years to recover from shoulder surgery. But by the time he was 53 he was back on top. The shoulders were pain free, he was remarried to his soul mate Perri Greenberg, who is his biggest fan and he was swimming as fast as he had in college.

The records began to tumble. And they haven't stopped. Today, Rich Abrahams owns 11 world and 22 American Masters records. He is one of a handful of Masters swimmers ever to hold world or American records simultaneously in three different age groups. What's more, his 50-54 mark for the 50 meter freestyle (24.75) is faster than the world record in the 45-49 age group. The same is true for his American records in the 50 yard free.

In 2005, his first year in the 60-64 age group, Abrahams simply annihilated the previous marks, ending the year with ten new American and four new world records. In the 100 yard butterfly, for example, only one man over 60 had ever broken one minute, and he'd done a 59.39. Abrahams hacked almost five seconds off that time with an astonishing 54.92. In the 100 yard freestyle, the American record, held by 1960 Olympic gold medalist Jeff Farrell, had stood at 52.03 for seven years, unapproachable, unassailable. Abrahams clocked 49.14 easily becoming the first man over 60 to break 50 seconds.

To put that time into perspective, consider that the 50 second barrier remained unbroken until 1944, when Alan Ford clocked 49.7. It was not until 1957 that an elite swimmer swam faster than Rich Abrahams at 60.

Abrahams even outdoes himself. In 2005, he blazed a 1:03.03 for 100 meters butterfly obliterating the previous record for men 60-64 by over four and a half seconds. Even more impressively, the time was almost a full second faster than his own, still-standing world record of 1:03.90 for men 55-59 set five years earlier!

Asked if he thinks he'll be able to break 50 seconds for 100 yards freestyle and a minute for 100 meters at age 65, Abrahams replies immediately, "I don't see why not."

How about 70? He hesitates, then replies, "That may be harder. We'll have to see."

Seventy five, anyone?

Rich was photographed November 4, 2005 in Denver, Colorado.
Profile contributed by Phil Whitten

Natalie Coughlin

In 1998, when 16 year old Natalie Coughlin won her first U.S. national swimming title, the talented and versatile swimmer seemed on the road to Olympic glory. She was called a swimming prodigy, a once-in-a-generation athlete, later a female Michael Phelps. She was compared with Olympic gold medalist Tracy Caulkins, one of the most versatile swimmers in history. But following a series of bumps in her road, Coughlin probably felt more like speedskater Dan Jansen, "the heartbreak kid" whose devastating and well documented setbacks left the world wondering if he was destined to be the best skater never to win Olympic gold. But Dan Jansen persevered and Coughlin did too although at times she got so frustrated and disappointed she almost quit swimming. The rest is history – Olympic history.

Natalie Coughlin was a water baby. Her mother Zennie swam when she was pregnant with Natalie and frequently tells reporters that Natalie was swimming "before she was born." At the time, Zennie and her husband Jim lived in Vallejo, California. The family had a pool in their back yard, and they often visited family in Hawaii, where little Natalie enjoyed splashing in the surf. She had her first swimming lessons when she was just ten months old, and at age six she competed in her first races with the neighborhood recreational swim team. Although she competed enthusiastically, her first race didn't exactly foreshadow her future success.

"My first race was the 25 fly," Coughlin remembers, "and I was disqualified because I was unable to get my arms out of the water during the last part of the race. My favorite event was probably the 25 back or free." Like most kids, Coughlin had her own pre-meet routine. "I would go to bed in my swimsuit, a size 34," says Coughlin, who now wears a more appropriately fitted size 28. "In the morning my mom would French braid my hair and put my cap on at the house. She would make me fried rice and eggs (a common Filipino breakfast) with a little soy sauce. It was my favorite and still is! When I got to the swim meet, I would put my goggles around my neck so that I wouldn't lose them. I wouldn't take my cap or goggles off until after my last race of the day."

At the time, few realized just how much potential she had – especially the official who DQ'd her. By the time she was 12, Coughlin started to become more serious about her swimming and when she was 13, she joined a more competitive group, the Terrapin Swim Team in Concord, California. She commuted 30 minutes in each direction to attend workouts twice a day, and added Saturday workouts to the routine. By the time she was 16, she had qualified for the U.S. Senior Nationals in every event of every distance from the 50 freestyle to the 400 individual medley, an unprecedented accomplishment in the history of USA Swimming. All her hard work was paying off, but the resulting media attention caught her a little off guard.

"I was so young I didn't really understand all the labels that were placed on me," says Coughlin, who was just two years old when Tracy Caulkins stood at the top of the Olympic podium. "The media attention steadily increased around that time, but I didn't actually notice the increase until it disappeared."

But she soon learned that fame is truly a "fickle food on a shifting plate." "I tore the labrum in my left shoulder in the spring of '99, and the media attention quickly disappeared," says Coughlin, who admitted taking a break from the media wasn't necessarily a bad thing. At the time, her shoulder often went numb during practice. So she didn't realize she'd hurt it until hours later, when she woke up in the middle of the night with a throbbing pain. The next morning, she couldn't lift her arm. The injury, which happened only a year before the 2000 U.S. Olympic Trials, was emotionally as well as physically devastating. Natalie Coughlin was expected to make the Olympic team in several events, but she was unable to train the way she had before the injury. That year, she failed to make the U.S. Olympic team and some thought the young swimming star was all washed up.

It seemed cruel after all her years of hard work. She endured intense physical therapy sessions focused on fixing structural problems in her body, and she did a lot of kicking workouts in the pool.

During her rehabilitation, Coughlin realized she needed more understanding and support from the people in her swimming circle. "It took about two years before I could train without pain," says Coughlin, "I hated swimming." Her rehabilitation routine gradually isolated her from the group. She needed a new environment, and her choice of college would soon offer an opportunity either to resurrect or end her swimming career.

"When I was deciding where to go to college I knew I wanted to stay in California," says Coughlin. "Academics were very important, so I looked at Cal, UCLA and Stanford." She was looking for a team environment that would allow her to feel more comfortable, and ultimately decided to join Coach Teri McKeever and the Golden Bears at Cal. "I wasn't sure how long I would swim, or even if I would make it all four years. I

felt that the team at Cal and Teri were very much like a family. Even if I was injured, I could be a part of the team."

As it turned out McKeever's leadership and the close-knit team atmosphere at Cal made all the difference in the world.

"Teri cares about her swimmers as if they we were her kids," says Coughlin. "She looks at us as people, rather than just her athletes, and she cares about what is going on in our lives, not just what's going to affect us in the pool." According to Coughlin, the team atmosphere helped ease the pressure she had been feeling, and that had a positive effect on her swimming. But most important McKeever allowed Coughlin to decide whether or not to continue swimming, and Coughlin says that's why she's still swimming today. "Because Teri left it up to me, I actually realized that I still do love the sport and that I want to continue with it."

It soon became abundantly clear that Coughlin would not only be part of the team, she would become one of the most celebrated individuals in the history of collegiate athletics. During her career at Cal, Coughlin won 12 NCAA titles – the second most career titles for a swimmer in NCAA women's championship history – and she went undefeated in dual meets over four years (61-0). She broke university, NCAA, American, U.S. Open and world records in several different events. She was honored as a three time Pac 10 and NCAA Swimmer of the Year from 2001-2003, she was chosen as the 2002 Female World Swimmer of the Year by "Swimming World Magazine" and she was recognized as the 2004 Female Collegiate Athlete of the Year by "Sports Illustrated".

Perhaps Coughlin's most dominant performance was at the 2002 NCAA Women's Swimming and Diving Championships in Austin, Texas which "Swimming World Magazine" recently called "the greatest exhibition of women's swimming in history." At the time and looking at films, the most unsettling thing about the whole display was how effortless it looked. During the competition Coughlin finished ridiculously far ahead of strong fields in every race, obliterating NCAA and American records in the 100 fly, both backstrokes and the 100 free. In the 100 fly, she lowered Jenny Thompson's American record from 51.07 to 50.01. In the 100 backstroke, she crushed her own record of 50.57 with a mind blowing time of 49.97 and in the 200 back, she lowered her own record from 1:50.90 to 1:49.52. Before Coughlin, those backstroke records were 52.71 held by Catherine Fox in the 100 and 1:52.98 held by Whitney Hedgepeth in the 200. To punctuate a stunning championship performance, Coughlin erased the newly minted American record in the 100 free with a leadoff swim from the 400 free relay.

Leading up to the 2004 Olympic Trials, everything seemed to be going very well for Coughlin. She was the world record holder in the 100 meter backstroke, and the first and only woman to break the magical one-minute barrier in that event (59.58). She was also the American record holder in the 100 meter freestyle (53.99) and 200 backstroke (2:08.53), and among the fastest active performers in the 100 fly (57.88). She also showed great promise in other events such as the 200 free, in which she held the short course yards American record (1:42.65).

The 2003 World Swimming Championship in Barcelona was supposed to confirm her as one of the world's next swimming superstars, but things didn't go exactly as planned. Just before the competition began, Coughlin came down with a high fever and couldn't perform up to her potential. She failed to make the semifinals in her signature event, the 100 backstroke, and failed to win a single individual medal.

"It was tough trying to compete with a 102-103 degree fever, but it was completely out of my control. Because I had no control over the situation – I couldn't have prevented it or done anything – I wasn't as upset as people expected me to be. Obviously I was really upset right after my 100 back, but I quickly got over it."

The setback left Coughlin with a difficult decision about what she would swim at the 2004 U.S. Olympic Trials.

"I chose the events that I was really passionate about and had confidence swimming," says Coughlin, who chose to swim the 50 and 100 freestyle and the 100 backstroke. Much to the surprise of many swimming fans, she decided not to swim the 200 back or the 200 free, events in which she was among the favorites for gold in Athens. Coughlin made the U.S. Olympic team in all three of her chosen events, which also secured her position as a leading contender for more medals on relays.

At the 2004 Olympics Coughlin won five medals, a bid for the most medals ever by a U.S. female athlete in one Olympiad. Her Olympic medals included gold in the 100 meter backstroke (1:00.37) and the 4x200 meter relay, silver in the 4x100 meter freestyle and medley relays and bronze in the 100 meter freestyle (54.40). A high point was her 200 meter leadoff split (1:57.74) on the world record setting 800 meter freestyle relay, a personal best and was faster than the gold medal winning time (1:58.03) in the 200 freestyle by Romania's Camelia Potec.

"I knew I had a good chance in that event," said Coughlin, "but because of my 100 back I couldn't swim both." That leadoff leg confirmed her belief that she could have won the individual event, but as Coughlin said, "I wouldn't have changed anything."

Although the Olympics validated Natalie Coughlin – the child prodigy, the heartbreak kid and the once-in-a-generation swimmer – in the world of swimming and athletics, the experience didn't really change her attitude towards the sport. That happened back in the pool at Berkeley, under the watchful eye of Teri McKeever and the change gave Natalie an insight that was perhaps the most important any athlete could ever receive.

"I was swimming for myself," says Coughlin. "I wasn't swimming because I felt like I had to swim. I was swimming because I actually enjoyed it."

Natalie was photographed January 12, 2006 in Kailua-Kona, Hawaii.
Profile contributed by Bill Volckening.

David Yudovin

David Yudovin shouldn't be alive right now. By all rights, the 55 year old from Cambria, California should have died in the shallow water off of the California coast in 1978, when he went into cardiac arrest at the end of a nine and a half hour swim from Anacapa Island. Or perhaps his end should have come in 1988 when David's doctors told him that he would die within two days from leukemia.

Determination has done more than keep David alive – it has made him one of the most accomplished long-distance channel swimmers in history. David, who lives with his wife Beth in their homes in California and Hawaii, has defied and beaten the odds by completing the trio of channel swims around the world: the English Channel, Catalina Island, and the Cook Strait. This last accomplishment made him the oldest swimmer to ever complete the 20 mile Cook Strait passage. He's also made several successful first swims in Asia, including the Sunda Strait in Indonesia, the Bali to Java passage and a 12 hour swim from Honchu Island to Hokkaido Island, Japan.

But David's swimming story really begins in 1978 in the shallow waters off the coast of Santa Barbara in Southern California, where David was hypothermic, unconscious and drowning after going into cardiac arrest at the end of his attempt to be the first to complete the swim from Anacapa Island to the mainland. It had been a cold swim, with water temperatures in the 50's. David's memory of the swim ends at the five hour mark. After more than nine hours of swimming through the cool water, David's body was becoming hypothermic. When he reached the relatively warmer water off the coast, his blood vessels, which had been restricting the flow of blood to his extremities, suddenly opened up. David had a heart attack and began to drown.

David arrived at the hospital "dead on arrival." He was in cardiac arrest for one hour and 15 minutes. Yet he survived.

"I was in intensive care and I woke up 24 hours later," David says. "My mom and my sister were there and I asked if I made the swim. They said, 'no, you didn't,' and I had a complete temper tantrum, ripped all the lines out, and really didn't realize what had happened to me until a team of doctors came into my room and said, 'we are always curious when there is a beyond-life experience.'"

From that point on, David says, he decided that he would never take any part of his life for granted. He finished the Anacapa attempt with pneumonia, cracked ribs, countless scars and he had nearly died, but the failure seemed to motivate David.

Four years later, after failing to make it across both the English Channel and again across Anacapa, he finally completed the Anacapa passage.

"It was unbelievable," he says. "When I came up on the beach I was in tears. I was absolutely bawling with elation."

Perhaps David was destined to greatness in the water. As an 11 year old surfing junkie in Southern California, he saw long-distance swimmers training out in the ocean – an experience that could qualify as a vision of his future.

"I'd be sitting out there on my board, waiting for the waves, and these swimmers would emerge, maybe out of the fog or I'd see them come up beyond the surf line with these heavy goggles on and caps," David says. "It was romantically mystical to me that these people would be swimming in the ocean like this."

Like many long-distance open water swimmers, David's goals have never been about speed. Instead, he decided to make his mark in swimming by being the first to complete various passages around the world. David is particularly proud that he currently has seven first completions to his name.

The most difficult of his open water swims was the Sunda Strait in 2000, which presented several unique challenges. First, the water temperature was between 84 and 86 degrees, which David says was like "swimming in a Jacuzzi." For such warm temperatures, he had to lose weight so that he could shed body heat faster. He also had to prepare for what would be a ten-and-a-half hour swim in "searing equatorial sun." The second challenge was the endless swarms of stinging jellyfish and the skin-scraping coral blooms. David spent four years training to swim the Sunda Strait and acclimating himself to the heat and the jellyfish stings. Even so, during his training for the attempt he was unsure if he could make it.

"How much of this can I take," he recalls asking himself. "I don't know. Nobody has done this before – this was truly out on the edge."

But he had prepared well and had trained and become friends with fishermen from a local Muslim village. When David first arrived at the village to train, he drove up in a black limousine with a chauffeur. The villagers looked at him and laughed. But David earned their respect immediately when the villagers saw his strong swimming stroke and serious approach to the endeavor. "Suddenly it went from, 'here is a loony American coming in to do something coo-coo,' to 'OK, this is real,'" he remembers.

On the day of the swim the local shaman blessed David and 11 fishermen accompanied him in their boats. The conditions were perfect, but there were so many jellyfish that David felt as if he was swimming through a woman's long hair. When he finished the Sunda Strait he was so swollen from the stings that he had to spend the night popping Benadryl.

Another significant accomplishment for David was his 10 mile swim from Nusa Penida to Bali in Indonesia in 1997. The importance of the swim wasn't so much that he was the first person to complete the dangerous, whirlpool-laden passage, but that his attempt created a wonderful moment of micro-diplomacy between local cultures. David had been training in Bali with the help of a group of Hindu fishermen, but the fishermen did not have a boat large enough to assist him on the full passage. Two local fishermen broke tradition and went to the neighboring Muslim village to ask for a larger boat. On the day of the swim two fishermen from the Hindu village and two fishermen from the Muslim village assisted, riding together in a boat, singing songs together, and celebrating together when David completed the swim.

"It took a common goal, and here were these diametrically opposed religions working together and saying, 'we're going to do this,'" David says. He still calls the Nusa Penida swim one of his more significant swims because of the cooperation that his swim initiated between the two villages.

David's near-death experiences were not limited to his Anacapa Island disaster. In 1988 doctors diagnosed David with leukemia. After a bike accident that year he contracted tetanus. The tetanus interacted with David's leukemia medicine to make him desperately ill. "I was given two days to live, I had a spleen the size of a football, a fever of 104, I couldn't eat, and I couldn't walk up the stairs of my house to go to bed." Again, David survived. He lost his spleen but kept his adventurous attitude.

For instance, in 1996 he finally completed the English Channel on his fourth attempt. David's first attempt at the historic passage had been in 1977, when, he says, he was a cocksure 26 year old who was "too cool for words." David had been sick that year and wasn't physically ready, and he had to give up halfway across the Channel. It was his first real failure as a swimmer. In 1980, after David had recovered from the Anacapa experience, he again failed in the Channel and, yet again, in 1985 the weather made passage impossible. But David swam for six hours in sideways sleet that year before giving in. Finally, in 1996, he cleared the Channel in thirteen-and-a-half hours, the second half of the swim through a rough storm. Looking back, David says that he was blessed that he didn't complete the Channel on his first attempt in 1977.

"It was amazing and humbling. When I look back to the 1977 English Channel swim I realize that it built me up to greater things. If I had succeeded then I might have stopped, like so many other people."

Though he has accomplished all of his major goals in swimming, including his induction into the International Marathon Swimming Hall of Fame in Fort Lauderdale, Florida in 2000, David says that he hopes to still be kicking through the surf when he's 90 years old. Ever since he was that 11 year old kid on the surfboard watching channel swimmers, the open water has been part of his life.

"There's something spiritual about being in the water to me," he says. "It puts my mind and my body in a completely different level. Even just taking a shower. Sometimes if I'm feeling frustrated or anxious about something I just go take a shower. It just soothes me."

David has officially retired from running the seafood storage and distribution company that he created, and he and Beth have been getting more involved in hands-on community service, which is how they originally met. But he is still committed to swimming, and perhaps he is improving in some ways. During the summer of 2006, to celebrate the 30th anniversary of his Catalina Island swim David attempted the 26 mile swim again. The conditions were terrible that night, but he got into the water anyway and began swimming. Two hours in he realized that he would never make it because of the conditions, but David continued on for another three hours and watched the sun come up before getting out of the water. As a younger swimmer he would have been torn up about not completing the swim, but now, he says, he completely enjoyed it.

"It is a wonderful thing to be my age, 55 going on 56, and I am more agile and more fit than when I was 17 years old. All my years of experience are directing me now. When it's right it's right, but when it's not right, that's when the wisdom kicks in. It was so cool to go five hours and not let it devastate me. I just came out and said, 'that was a wonderful five hour swim.'"

David was photographed January 10, 2006 off the coast of Wailea-Maui, Hawaii. Profile contributed by Jeremy Shweder.

Jenny Thompson

Jenny Thompson's swimming career has been turned inside out, put under the spotlight and dissected as thoroughly as her powerful strokes. Winning 12 Olympic medals, most of any American in history, tends to erode a person's anonymity. There are also Jenny's world records, set unusually far apart in 1992 and 1999, and her numerous comebacks during a career that began in 1987 and ended 17 years later.

Jenny's swimming accomplishments go on and on. For example: she has won 85 medals in international competitions, making her the most decorated swimmer in history. "Sports Illustrated" named Jenny as one of the greatest 100 female athletes of the 20th century. She is only the third female swimmer ever to qualify for four Olympic Games. And the list continues.

Not every moment has been blessed for the charismatic swimmer from New England. Although she was often favored to win individual golds in international competition, only two of Jenny's 12 medals are from the solo events. But while most Olympic athletes have one, maybe two Olympics to make their mark, Jenny Thompson has just kept going – and winning. In the world of competitive swimming her name is one of the best recognized, in part because she swam – and won medals, including eight golds – in every Olympics from 1992 to 2004. Jenny has always been a fierce competitor, but the key to her longevity, she says, is that she never let herself get too invested in the sport. "I've been able to keep things in perspective and keep balance in my life," Jenny says. "In doing that I've been able to not get burned out emotionally with the sport. I think I've always been able to maintain my love for it."

"As you get older, life gets harder and there are more stresses. More and more swimming is sort of a safe place, a place where I can get all my anxieties or frustrations with life out. It helps me emotionally."

Jenny ended her swimming career with typical flourish by winning the two silver medals in the 2004 Athens Olympics that gave her the record for most medals by an American. Upon leaving Greece Jenny returned to her second career, one that she put on hold while she trained for her final Olympics. Jenny started medical school at Columbia University in New York City in 2001 and is now a doctor. She began school just days before the 9/11 attacks and watched in horror from her dorm room window as the Twin Towers burned. Jenny had taken a break from swimming and was considering retirement after 2000, but she was drawn back to competition not long after the attacks.

"After 9/11 there was a feeling of 'what can I do to help?'" she says. "This feeling of 'what can I do?' And then just thinking back on my life, swimming is the way that I've best been able to inspire people or give hope. So that was part of the reason for coming back."

Jenny was always a natural swimmer, and according to family legend she could swim before she could walk. But Jenny was a strong athlete in several sports, and she jokes that she would have been "much richer" if she had stuck with tennis lessons as child and become a professional tennis player rather than a professional swimmer. Jenny had a strong connection with the water from an early age, however, and she recognized that she was talented in the pool. When she was 12 years old she was the only person on her team to qualify for the junior national competition, where she placed sixth. "I think we knew at that point that OK, things are going very well," Jenny says. "After that is when we moved to New Hampshire. I never really thought very far into the future, like Olympics or anything. I just wanted to keep improving."

Jenny certainly kept improving. She won her first international gold medal in the 50 meter freestyle at the 1987 Pan American Games as a 14 year old, then went on to Stanford University and helped lead its powerhouse swimming team. During her four years at Stanford the swim team went undefeated and won every meet, conference competition and NCAA title. She set individual world records in 1992 and again in 1999, with the latter breaking a seemingly untouchable 18 year old mark in the 100 meter butterfly. Jenny says that when she looks back, the aspect of her swimming career that stands out most is how long she was able to stay at the top of her sport.

"If I think of it now, I guess my longevity, the level that I was able to maintain for many years is the thing that I feel most proud of. I guess that being able to break the world record – I broke one in '92 in another one in '99 – to have that kind of space between two different world records in two different events, I think that's pretty cool."

One of Jenny's inspirations was her mother, Margrid, who raised Jenny and her three brothers by herself. After moving the family to New Hampshire from the Boston area so Jenny could train with the best coaches, Margrid continued to commute 90 minutes to work every day in Boston.

"She's always been an extremely strong and independent woman," Jenny says of her mother. "She raised four kids by herself. When I was a kid it never fazed me that she was doing that. But I can't imagine how hard that was, that she was working full time, raised

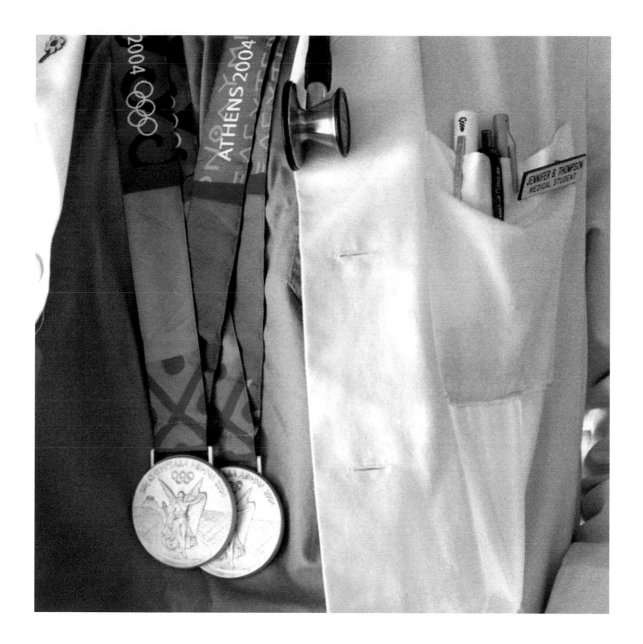

four kids really well, I might add, and was still spending a lot of time with us."

Margrid, who had survived growing up in WWII Germany, was a rock in Jenny's life and swimming career. In early 2004, however, Margrid died after a battle with esophageal cancer before the Athens Olympics, Jenny's last. "It was a very exciting Olympics for me and very sentimental, and sort of nostalgic, because I knew that I was going to retire," she says. "I think it was difficult for me as well. I have to say that the Trials and the Olympics were harder, not having her there."

After retiring from competitive swimming, Jenny put her focus into her medical studies. She says that she was drawn to medicine because it provided a direct way to affect people's lives. After graduation from medical school in 2006 she began a one year internship at Memorial Sloan-Kettering Medical Center in New York and in the summer of 2007 Jenny will become an anesthesiology resident at Brigham and Women's Hospital in Boston.

"I really like that you're there for someone in their most elemental needs – their health," Jenny says of her new career. "I just really enjoy people, hearing their stories, being able to help them in crisis. It's never the same, minute to minute. Every day is so different. It can get very stressful, but also it's so gratifying."

Jenny was photographed December 18, 2004 in New York City, New York.
Profile contributed by Jeremy Shweder.

Melanie Benn

When 18 year old Melanie Benn headed home to San Diego for Christmas break during her freshman year at Humboldt State University in 1995, she thought she was getting the flu.

She never could have imagined that days later, she would be facing the loss of her forearms and legs above the knees because of bacterial meningitis, a relatively rare but critical infectious disease that causes inflammation of the membranes surrounding the brain and spinal chord.

She also couldn't have imagined that a decade later, she would have completed a career as a world class swimmer, competed around the globe and also earned a Masters degree and embarked on a busy career as a social worker in a prestigious medical research institution.

Benn had been feeling sick and run down for about a week before her trip home that Christmas. By the time she reached her family on Christmas Eve, she was vomiting and then fell unconscious. She would be in the hospital for five months, battling the infection and a related blood clotting disorder that caused gangrene in her extremities and necessitated the quadruple amputation.

Benn's obvious poise, warmth and self confidence make it easier to understand how she rebounded from such a devastating and sudden illness. She exudes relaxed humor and modesty over her accomplishments; and in a wheelchair and prostheses she balances a work, training and personal schedule that would overwhelm many able-bodied people.

She claims to be a "big wimp" when it comes to sports. "I'm not an athlete at heart," she says. But her success in the pool, and the way she rebuilt her life with a disability, reveal what could only be described as remarkable toughness and determination.

Before she contracted meningitis, Benn had never heard of it. Close to 3,000 Americans a year contract viral meningitis or the more serious bacterial form of the disease, and it is more likely to spread in crowded living conditions such as college campuses. The symptoms of its onset are similar to those of the flu but include rashes and a stiff neck. Though it is not widely known, there is a vaccine for meningitis that costs about $65. The U.S. Centers for Disease Control and Prevention (CDC) now recommend that all adolescents get the vaccine, as young as age 11 or at least before they enter college. Benn's mother Candie has become an active proponent of the vaccine and is a cofounder of the National Meningitis Association. Melanie has also done public awareness-raising and advocacy for the vaccine, and the company which manufactures it funded her family to cheer her on in Sydney and Athens at the 2000 and 2004 Paralympic Games.

"Because meningitis is kind of rare, it's taken a long time for awareness to come about," she says of the disease. "But there are a lot of risk factors for people living in close proximity, like kids at boarding schools or sports camps."

Along with the amputations, Benn also needed a kidney transplant, from her father Ed, and spent a year on dialysis. Her recovery was rough, needless to say, but she says the support and positive attitude of her family and friends helped her through it.

"People are able to survive experiences like that because you regress emotionally," she says. "I remember being itchy, tired, hungry. You don't analyze what your life is going to be like from here on. You turn to the people around you for emotions. During the really acute days when I was getting amputations and dialysis and skin grafts, my friends were always there, ordering pizzas and laughing, really upbeat. I'm sure it was hard for them to be like that, but they did it. When they talked it was always like 'when you go back to school, when you do this or that' – it was never a question."

Benn didn't waste any time going back to school, she started classes at a local community college while her bandages were still on. Then she transferred to San Diego State University and graduated with a degree in psychology. Later she earned a Masters in social work at UCLA, and started working at the University of California at San Diego (UCSD) medical school as a counselor for hospital patients, including those with HIV and AIDS and postpartum mothers.

"It's a broad range, mostly crisis situations," she said. "I love being in the medical center, the environment is really conducive to learning. I was a patient at UCSD so having that experience gives me more insight as a provider of care."

In high school Benn played softball and basketball and was on the diving team. "The swimmers hated us because we were bad and brought the team score down," she laughs. "We even had to ride in a separate bus from the swimmers."

During the year of dialysis following her illness, she had a port in her chest for the procedure that prevented her from getting in the water. But once that was over, she took the advice of several friends and hopped back in the pool.

"I absolutely loved it," she said. "At the time I was still learning to use these arms and legs (prostheses) and in a big wheelchair. I felt so cumbersome, so to be able to take everything off, to be able to move so freely just felt great. Sports had been a big part of my upbringing. After my illness, I wasn't sure what sport it would be. I had always done team sports, but swimming as an individual sport has really nurtured my sense of individuality. As a person with a disability that's important because you have to have a lot of strength."

Benn got psyched to start swimming while watching a fundraiser for the Challenged Athletes Foundation called the San Diego Triathlon Challenge at La Jolla Cove, a famous picturesque swimming spot. She started training for the following year's triathlon, and joined a local Masters swim team coached by Alan Voisard. She credits Voisard with convincing her to start competing, but he says she needed little encouragement.

"She asked me if I thought she could do this, and I said sure," said Voisard. "She was ready to go. We started with fins to help her feel the acceleration in the water. With shortened limbs it's harder to get that momentum going, but once she got the feel of it we weaned her off them."

He isn't surprised how quickly Benn progressed.

"She was very determined," he says. "Once she got in the water and had an idea of what the possibilities in swimming were for her, she stayed really committed, found her balance, the moments in swimming that would help her grow. She'd be doing flips in the water, messing around between sets, I think she enjoyed that sense of playfulness and freedom of movement that she didn't have (out of the water) at that point in her life."

Benn found out about the Paralympics, an international competition held immediately after the Olympic Games in the same venue. Athletes are grouped into categories based on their disability. Physical disabilities are rated on a scale of 1 to 10 based on mobility, Benn is in category 4. Categories 11-13 are for visually impaired athletes. Each event is held separately for each category.

At the Paralympic Games trials in Indianapolis in June 2000, Benn surprised herself by setting a national record in the 50 meter backstroke and a time in the 50 meter freestyle that ranked third in the world.

So she was off to Sydney, spending three weeks in the Olympic Village with athletes from around the world. She describes the Sydney experience, where she won a bronze medal on the 4x50 freestyle relay, as "amazing."

"It was really impressive just to be around that caliber of athletes from all different countries," she says. "You get on the bus in 'USA-land' and then go through 'Germany' and the 'Czech Republic' and other countries, more and more people would get on. It was something to see eight wheelchairs trying to fit into a small space, communicating with hand signals and different languages. My favorite thing was seeing how the blind athletes would all get around with their hands on each other's shoulders."

"And with my social work background, it was interesting to see what kind of equipment people from different countries had and how they interacted. The swimmers from South America had nothing (in terms of modern prostheses or movement aids). One guy would go around on an old BMX bike, instead of a wheelchair. He'd ride right up to the blocks on it."

Four years later she qualified for the 2004 Paralympic Games in Athens, another experience she can best describe as "amazing." She thinks she performed better there, even though she had been training on her own rather than with a team because of her busy schedule. She won a silver in the 50 meter freestyle, bronze in the 100 meter freestyle and bronze in the 20 point 4x50 meter freestyle relay.

"I did better for having been there before and having more training and experience," she notes.

By the fall of 2005, Benn had turned in her "retirement papers" and removed herself from the mandatory random drug testing pool, which all potential Paralympic athletes must agree to.

"The drug testing process alone is enough to make you want to retire," she laughs. "They showed up at my house six hours after I'd gotten home from Athens and all I wanted to do was sleep."

She and her partner recently bought a condo in the Tierrasanta neighborhood of San Diego, not far from the medical center. She still swims, but just for fun, which has made her appreciate the sport in new ways, and she enjoys doing yoga and camping and has experimented with sailing. "I like to keep a balance of my career, my family life, my spirituality," she said. "But I am looking for a new sport. I'm not sure what it will be yet."

Voisard is confident she'll succeed in whatever she does, athletically or otherwise.

"She is very humble, she's not a limelight person, but she's a star," he says. "She's like a magnet when she enters a room. She's so charming, because people see the authentic person there."

Melanie was photographed July 31, 2005 in San Diego, California.
Profile contributed by Kari Lydersen.

Terry Laughlin

This 54 year old has taught thousands of adults how to swim as the founder and Director of Total Immersion Swimming. Terry Laughlin of New Paltz, NewYork has coached swimmers for over 30 years, written hundreds of articles, and published books and videos, although his own introduction to the sport anything but auspicious.

Laughlin's family used to go to Bar Beach, in Port Washington on Long Island Sound. There, his father tried to teach him how to swim.

"I think I was a pretty difficult student," says Laughlin. There was a raft about 20 yards offshore, and to the young Laughlin, reaching it seemed a nearly unattainable goal. "I remember practicing dead-man's float quite a bit until I began to get a sense that I might not sink," he laughs. "Then I added arms and legs and was moving. I have no recollection of how long it took me to get to that raft, but it felt like quite a triumph to do so." Laughlin has an old home movie of himself, age about 10, swimming across the width of a pool during a summer vacation. "I beat the water within an inch of its life. Head up and whipping back and forth, arms windmilling wildly, the water churned to a froth."

In 1964, when Laughlin was 13, he tried out for the CYO swim team in his parish. It was what he calls "the lowest level of competitive swimming you can imagine." The tryout involved swimming the width of a 6 lane pool. "One of the coaches dove in and went after me after watching me swim a few strokes, thinking I'd need saving," Laughlin remembers. "He didn't manage to catch me, but I still flunked the tryout." So, his first competitive experience was a Rotary Club sponsored meet when he was 14. "I can recall my time exactly, 19.2 sec for a 25 free and I got a medal for placing 2nd in 13-14 boys."

When Laughlin was in 10th grade at St. Mary's High School in Manhasset, New York the school started a swim team and Laughlin joined.

"Brother Ronald, our coach would spend the first 10 minutes of our precious hour exhorting us to greater 'spirit'," says Laughlin, "and we'd spend the rest of the session swimming repeat 25's in waves from each end of the pool. Dive in, swim to the other end. Climb out. Repeat. I was always one of the slowest, which confirmed for me that I was 'slow.'" Despite his lack of obvious aptitude for swimming it fascinated him more than any other sport. His local library had a book about swimming – just one book. It was written by Dave Armbruster, published decades earlier, and Laughlin checked it out repeatedly in search of new insight and understanding.

Laughlin began to gain this new insight and understanding during the Christmas holidays, when Adelphi College All-American distance swimmer Tom Liotti came to run a workout as a guest coach. He instructed the group to start with a 500, and explained circle swimming to them.

"I'm sure it was a mess," said Laughlin, "but I realized about eight or ten lengths into it that I was passing people for the first time in my life. It finally dawned on me I might not be slow after all. I might just need a longer distance to hit my stride."

Liotti later made it possible for Laughlin to get his first coaching job. When Liotti received a late admission to Delaware Law School in July 1972, he needed to find someone right away to take his place as the coach of the swimmers at the U.S. Merchant Marine Academy in Kings Point. Laughlin had just graduated from St. Johns two months earlier. Although he was only 21, had no coaching experience and had not particularly distinguished himself as a swimmer, Liotti took him in to the Athletic Director and convinced him to hire Laughlin.

"My first season was a revelation," said Laughlin. "Though I knew nothing about technique or training, I used my instincts from my training experiences in college, concentrated on doing the things I'd found engaging, and minimized the stuff I'd found boring." For example, when his sprinters persisted in repeating 1:13 for 10x100 on 1:30, Laughlin told them they could swim 10x100 on any interval they liked, but only those under a minute would count toward the total. More importantly, Laughlin acted on his instincts about the aesthetics of swimming. After watching great swimmers and realizing they looked better than other swimmers in the water, Laughlin set out to teach swimmers how they should look. He felt that approach had potential, and he was right. At the conference championship at season's end, his team won every freestyle event in record time, and Laughlin was voted Coach of the Year. "That was the first thing I'd ever done in my life that had the effect of impressing others."

Following his early days coaching swimming, Laughlin met Bill Boomer, former coach at the University of Rochester and technical consultant for Stanford University. According to Laughlin, Boomer "planted the intriguing idea that the 'shape of the vessel' might have just as much influence as the 'size of the engine' on a swimmer's performance." Although Laughlin had been doing the same thing somewhat intuitively, Boomer's ideas helped him crystallize his approach to teaching swimming. After a few more years during which Laughlin worked primarily as a writer, Total Immersion Swimming was born. Since then, Laughlin has written books, produced videos, and conducted clinics all across the map. But since then, not a day has passed that he's failed to give thanks for being allowed to find his metier at such a young age.

Terry was photographed August 4, 2005 in New Paltz, New York.
Profile contributed by Bill Volckening.

Maritza Correia

Facing a medical challenge, she found a way to overcome. Facing personal strife, she gained strength. Staring at history, she knocked down previously impenetrable walls. In every way, Maritza Correia has persevered, along the way developing from a scoliosis-afflicted youngster into one of the premier sprint freestyle swimmers in the world.

Her background hardly laid the groundwork for an illustrious career in the pool. Because of its training requirements, swimming tends to be embraced more by the financially blessed. Maritza, born to parents from Guyana, a small nation located in the northern portion of South America, spent the first eight years of her life in Puerto Rico. She is also of black heritage, not typically connected to swimming excellence. Somehow, though, she overachieved.

As a 6 year old, Maritza received her introduction to competitive swimming when she was diagnosed with scoliosis, a condition that causes curvatures to the spine. Doctors determined that Maritza's spine was 15 degrees off center. She had a choice: swimming or gymnastics. Through athletics, she would be able to enhance her flexibility and, with good posture, correct her condition.

Maritza opted for the water and as a 7 year old began taking swimming lessons in the backyard of a local man who instructed several youths from her neighborhood. Almost instantly she demonstrated a gift for sprinting. She also possessed the competitive desire necessary for a future Olympian. One afternoon, during an impromptu relay race, Maritza had given her team an early advantage and was waiting for a 4 year old to finish off the triumph. So, when the younger swimmer hesitated before plunging into the water, Maritza provided support in the form of a well-timed shove. Call the move an indicator of her desire.

Shortly after she won a gold medal in the 50 freestyle in the Puerto Rican equivalent of the Junior Olympics, Correia and her family relocated to Tampa, Florida. Eventually, a stellar high school swimming career blossomed and her name was whispered about on pool decks throughout the Sunshine State. A black woman in a predominantly white sport, Correia was storming toward barricades never before breached.

Recruited by the University of Georgia, a national power program in the collegiate ranks, Correia began making a name for herself on the national swimming scene shortly after she arrived on the Athens campus. Heading into the 2000 Olympic Trials, a black

female swimmer had never represented the United States on the grandest stage in sports and Maritza had that chance. But she failed to advance out of the preliminaries of the 100 freestyle.

That year Anthony Ervin earned an Olympic invitation to Sydney, but Maritza will forever be known as the first American female from her race to compete in the quadrennial Games. It happened four years later. Competing in Long Beach, California, Maritza qualified for the Athens Olympics in the 400 freestyle relay, thanks to a fourth place finish in the 100 freestyle. A month later, she earned a silver medal at the Olympics in relay duty. Representing her country is an accomplishment she takes much pride in, along with becoming the first woman of color to hold an American record. That achievement arrived in the 50 freestyle at the 2002 NCAA Championships.

Maritza, who is under contract to NIKE, has used her story to inspire when she is speaking to youths who attend inner city schools or are being held in detention centers. She emphasizes that swimming can provide opportunities similar to those she has been

afforded. She also discusses a never-give-up approach, the one she adopted after the 2000 Olympic Trials left her short of her goals.

One of her primary goals is to elevate the participation of minorities in the sport. She isn't looking to find international standouts. Maritza is aware that many minorities do not know how to swim and knows providing lessons would mean a safer environment when those individuals are around water. Of course, if a few minority swimmers find acclaim similar to that of Maritza's, well, that would be a bonus.

There was a time when Maritza, despite her inarguable talent, considered walking away from the pool. Like many athletes, particularly those who demonstrated great potential at a young age, Correia endured extreme pressure from her father, Vincent, a mechanical engineer. A proponent of mental toughness, the family's patriarch held his daughter to a strict academic-study schedule, a decision that Maritza does not regret. What she does regret, however, is the verbal abuse that was unleashed.

During high school, after Maritza failed to emerge victorious at the Florida State

Championships, Vincent's words pushed her to the brink. Is it worth the anguish? Why is my father, a man who should provide endless support, hammering my psyche? These were questions that upset Maritza. They were questions that drove her toward quitting. Fortunately, she says, her mother Anne, a head nurse coordinator, has been ultra supportive throughout her life.

Her father's cruel words continued to torment Maritza even after she graduated from high school, particularly after the 2000 Olympic Trials. Vincent has called his daughter a disgrace to the family. Frequently not on speaking terms with her father, Maritza needed to take action. Finally, she sat at the computer and drafted an e-mail. She expressed her disappointment in his approach and, for the first time in her life, stood up for herself. After three days of contemplation, Maritza finally hit the send button. It was a cathartic moment.

Maritza, who received her degree in sociology from Georgia in December 2005, is a firm believer that God designed a specific plan for her. It is a plan that featured adversity – physical and emotional – but adversity that was meant to help her grow as a person.

Once a young child with a severe spinal condition, Maritza Correia has become a role model in the swimming community, especially to competitors of ethnic backgrounds. Knocked down following the 2000 Olympic Trials, she picked herself up and broke a barrier. She has shown that swimming is not just for the affluent or white sect. Simply, she has positioned herself as a living inspiration, proof that determination and focus can go a long way.

Maritza was photographed October 27, 2005 at the Brandon Sports & Aquatic Center in Tampa, Florida.

Profile contributed by John Lohn.

George Brunstad

On August 29, 2004 George Brunstad swam the English Channel. He started in Dover, England at 9:13 on the morning of August 28th, and landed on Sangatte Beach, south of Calais, France at 2:12 on the morning of the 29th. His swim was 15 hours and 59 minutes – twice the time of the listed record of 7 hours 17 minutes set by American Chad Hundeby in 1994. But George Brunstad established an extraordinary record of his own. Brunstad, was celebrating his 70th birthday which had been three days earlier and his swim made him the oldest person ever to swim the English Channel.

"The swim was a life affirming and life changing experience," said Brunstad. "There are a few high points in a person's life. For me, marriage to my wife Judy, the birth of our five children and ten grandchildren stand out." What he considers his biggest life changing experience was spiritual – when he became a Christian, in his words "making Christ the Master" of his life.

The English Channel is an arm of the Atlantic Ocean between western France and southern England. It opens into the North Sea, and the 21 mile Strait of Dover is its narrowest point. The first person to swim the channel was Matthew Webb in 1875. In 1926, Gertrude Ederle became the first woman to accomplish the feat. At the time, she broke the listed men's record by two hours. Until 2004, the oldest person to swim the English Channel was 67 year old Australian Clifford Batt in 1987, and the oldest woman was 57 year old American Carol Sing in 1999. Swimming across the bone chilling, often choppy Strait of Dover is less common than climbing to the top of Mount Everest. And like Everest, the English Channel has claimed its share of lives.

Until recently, the idea of a 70 year old completing the endurance swim was practically unthinkable, but it was also just the type of adventure George Brunstad relished most. In his younger days, he piloted B-52 bombers in the Air Force, then was a career commercial pilot for American Airlines. When he retired at age 60, he purchased a MiG-17 fighter plane and performed in air shows flying at speeds up to Mach 1.1 and pulling up to 9 Gs. But he didn't limit his love of the blue yonder to the stratosphere. Since his retirement, Brunstad has participated in long distance open water swimming events all over the United States and internationally.

The idea of swimming the English Channel first came to him in a dream. He saw himself as a 90 year old regretting his missed opportunity to have swum the English Channel.

He thinks a conversation he had had with eight-time Channel swimmer Thomas Hetzel may have triggered the dream.

"I asked him who was the oldest across the Channel and he told me of Bertram Clifford Batts of Australia in 18+ hours in 1987. I envisioned that the opportunity had been there and I had not acted upon it and the chance was gone forever. I woke up the next morning troubled and regretful." But as Walt Disney said in one of Brunstad's favorite inspirational quotes, "If you can dream it, you can do it." "When asked at my 69th birthday, 'What would you want to do that would be significant on your 70th birthday?' I answered, 'Swim the English Channel!'"

His family was enthusiastic, except for his wife Judy who was alarmed by the idea. "She was sitting with her arms crossed, frowning and shaking her head. I said, 'It doesn't look like Judy likes this idea!' Her answer was, 'Why would you want to do this? To boost your ego?" But when he started talking about the idea of doing the whole thing for charity, Judy started to reconsider. The couple had recently visited an organization in Hinche, Haiti, the Center for Hope which aims to build a church, orphanage, school and medical clinic for residents. They quickly settled on that cause, and George dedicated his swim to the Center for Hope. He raised $11,000 prior to the swim and over $50,000 since. He gives much of the credit to his wife.

"Judy became a driving force in the solicitation of some 250 sponsors in the raising of over $50,000 in behalf of the project," he says proudly.

Brunstad was confident in the water and had no apprehension because he was well prepared. "I had the right counsel, the right purpose and the right training." Although his longest training swim was 14 miles and seven hours long, he trained in 55-60 degrees (fahrenheit) water in Maine for three weeks prior to going to England. He also jogged for 20 minutes in 55 degrees water under the shower after workouts. "The water temperature was 63 degrees mid channel, a little colder on the British side," Brunstad reports.

From Brunstad's standpoint, his spiritual preparation was as crucial as his physical training. He kept a journal of inspirational sayings, had several Christian hymns and key scriptures on his mind, and hundreds of people praying for him.

"I was absolutely resolved to finish the swim," said Brunstad. "I just could not disappoint all those people who had faith in me and were counting on me. I prayed, others prayed and there were several prayer vigils ongoing during the swim."

Although he calls himself "a person with ordinary talent," George Brunstad's swim across the English Channel was extraordinary especially the finish at Sangatte. He knew he was getting close when he saw the glowing light sticks of escort swimmers Allison Streeter and Marcy MacDonald – both Channel swimming legends in their own right.

"I looked up and could make out some buildings and could see some surf. Then my left hand struck sand! The three of us ran up the beach and I threw my hands in the air and shouted 'Thank you Lord! God is great! Praise the Lord.' We joined hands with arms raised facing the boat's floodlight as the nine others shouted and celebrated."

George was photographed June 17, 2005 on Jennings Beach in Fairfield, Connecticut. Profile contributed by Bill Volckening.

Christopher Swain

During his 1,243 mile journey down the length of the Columbia River in the Pacific Northwest in 2003, Christopher Swain swam through 7 foot waves that left him struggling to keep the top antennae on his police escort boat in sight, navigated around dangerous, knockout-sized floating logs that bobbed, almost invisibly, slightly below the surface, and gargled hydrogen peroxide solution during his brief, in-water swim breaks to kill the bacteria that he swallowed with every breath in the river.

And somewhere along those 1,243 miles Christopher realized that he was no longer the same person that he had been when he began his quest to become the first person to swim the entire length of the Columbia. His swim was neither crazy nor impossible, but something that he had to do. At that point, Christopher was reborn in a way.

"I got the sense that I didn't really belong to me anymore," the 39 year old says about how he felt when he returned home to Burlington, Vermont. "A little bit of me belonged to the water now, and the river now. My wife sensed it right away. She said I have a mistress now, and it's the river."

Ever since that first long distance swim in the Pacific Northwest in 2003 to raise awareness of the health of the river and the people living along it, Christopher has dedicated much of his free time to environmental activism. Christopher has completed "clean water" swims along the 315 mile Hudson River in New York, the 129 miles of Vermont's Lake Champlain and the 80 miles of the Charles River in Massachusetts. The rivers and lakes that Christopher swims in are often chocolate colored and filled with chemical pollutants, gigantic tractor tires, sharp metallic chunks, and tons of everyday trash. And not only does he have to avoid the various objects in the water and swim for so many days in a row, he also has to navigate rapids in some stretches. For this he wears body armor to protect himself from smashing his limbs on rocks.

Christopher's next swim may be his most challenging. In 2007 he plans to begin a 1,000 mile swim along the East Coast of the United States starting in Ottawa, Canada, cutting across to the Atlantic Ocean, then following the Atlantic Coast to Washington, D.C.. The goal of this swim is to advocate for healthy oceans, and it will present unique difficulties, Christopher says, because the water is colder than the rivers he typically swims in, the tides and currents are a much bigger factor, and swimming through salt water is harder on a person's body. Also, unlike most of his river swims, he won't be near the land if he gets into trouble. The East Coast swim should take him three years, spaced out over the warmer seasons.

Christopher's affair with water started when he was a child in Massachusetts. His parents taught him to sail, row, and swim when he was very young. "As a boy I was the kid whose mother had to crack the whip to get him out of the water," he says. "I definitely remember my mom and my dad saying, 'C'mon, let's go.' I was just finding every excuse to stay in the ocean or the pool. I was happy there from an early age."

Despite attending the liberal and activist minded Wesleyan College, Christopher wasn't interested in political causes as a college student. Instead he rowed on the crew team, raced his bicycle and was "totally in his own zone," he says.

But eventually a desire to do something both personally challenging and meaningful with his life led Christopher back to the water, and it was the subject of clean water that captivated him. In 1996 he realized he could bring water quality to the public's attention after he had finished a 200 mile swim down the Connecticut River. He had organized the swim to bring attention to international human rights and, specifically, to the Universal

Declaration of Human Rights, a United Nations document which Christopher felt that not enough people were aware about.

"People in the media were happy to give me my 10 seconds to talk about universal human rights, but they were obviously there to do a story that some crazy idiot was swimming in there. And the next logical question after, 'Why are you doing that?' was, 'What's in the water? Do you know what's in the water?' They wanted to talk about water quality and pollution. And I remember filing that away in my mind, thinking, 'Well that would be something to do, swim for the river.'"

That first swim eventually led Christopher to the Columbia River, which led to the Hudson, then on to Lake Champlain. A typical day in the Hudson or Columbia rivers involved six hours of swimming, broken into 600 stroke segments. Christopher counts each stroke he takes. When he reaches 600 he pauses for food and rest. On good days he'll complete 9,000 to 11,000 strokes. Some days, when the current is rough or when he's not feeling strong, 6,000 strokes is all he manages. While Christopher isn't necessarily a fast swimmer, what separates him from many other strong swimmers is his ability to keep going in almost any condition. Ice cold snowmelt? Swim through it. Fifty mph winds? Find a way. Raw sewage on the Hudson or Lamprey eel attacks in Lake Champlain? All part of the challenge.

"There's a part of me that really responds to a challenge on the water because I believe that I have a good relationship with the water," he says. "The worse things get, the more I see it as a challenge to try to blend, or to find a rhythm, or to find a way through it."

Swimming those thousands of miles, Christopher learned to stop fighting the water. He says that every time he steps into a river he's offering himself to the waterway, understanding that it could be his last swim.

"In a way it makes it more peaceful because I'm not out there afraid I'm going to die," he says. "Like everyone, I'm afraid of getting seriously injured and all the little things that can happen. I've really been able to come to some understanding with myself that I might not make it. That means when I'm in these bad situations, I think I'm more alive and I'm more on my own side because I'm not spending energy worrying about getting killed."

Most days when he's in the water, Christopher feels it's "51 percent worth it." His swims take him away from his two daughters for weeks at a time, and he and his wife recently got divorced. Even when he's on a river swim, he keeps an exhausting schedule, speaking at schools about clean water or organizing his support crew and the next day's six hour swim. But then there are the moments when school kids line a bridge to cheer Christopher on during a swim or when the light hits the water at just the right angle, and then Christopher feels he's right where he's meant to be, making a connection to the river and bringing the cause of clean water to the public.

"In my mind I think I should spend less time in the water, spending more time with kids, anchoring projects," he says. "But the other part of me says that you can keep this up. It's a helpful gesture to be in the water, it totally works. So where's it going to go? I will swim more waterways. And I'll keep racking my brains for ways to make the waterways more friends. And I'll do things with an eye toward what my deeds and my work will look like to a younger version of myself."

Chris was photographed on August 23, 2005 on the banks of the Charles River in Boston, Massachusetts.

Profile contributed by Jeremy Shweder.

Dave Denniston

You know those two minute "Up Close" vignettes TV networks show to "personalize" an Olympic athlete about whom viewers may know nothing?

The ones that dramatize, some skeptics would say over dramatize, the challenges the athlete has had to face, the barriers he's overcome, the injuries and tragedies that have threatened to pull him down and end his career. They're designed to make you care about the athlete, to want to root for him.

Invariably they conclude: yes, he's faced down and overcome these challenges, and now here he is in (you fill in the city), ready to compete for Olympic glory in the finals of (you fill in the event).

Fade to the Olympic pool or stadium and the introduction of the finalists.

Well, by and large, and allowing for the writers' and producers' artistic license, these vignettes contain some truth. But what they leave out, what they fail to mention, are the dozens or even hundreds of equally talented, equally motivated other competitors. Athletes who overcame their own challenges, disappointments, injuries and tragedies, but fell just short of making the Olympic Team.

This is the story of one such athlete, a talented, intelligent, hard working, intense, funny, well coached swimmer who had all the tools he needed to make the U.S. Olympic Swim Team, but who fell just a few tenths of a second shy of achieving his dream. The story of a young man who eventually had to confront his own Olympian-size challenge, and had to do it alone, without the lights and cameras and cheering crowds.

This is the story of David Denniston.

As a kid growing up in the wide open spaces of Wyoming, not exactly the hottest spot on swimming's geological map, Dave had to travel 40 miles each way to get to and from swim practice. He showed promise, but his opportunities to develop that promise were strictly limited.

That all changed dramatically when his family moved to Littleton, Colorado in 1995 and Dave enrolled as a sophomore at Arapahoe High. There he blossomed under the skillful tutelage of George Fernandez, Arapahoe High and Greenwood Tiger Sharks' club coach and they dropped Dave's time for the 100 yard breaststroke from 1:01 to 57.1.

That summer he made the 1996 National Junior Team that competed in France. But the trip caused Dave to miss the state high school championships, so as he entered his senior year, Dave's best time remained 57.1 and only the University of Arizona had shown any interest in the skinny kid from Colorado.

Until the following February, when he went to the U.S. Winter Nationals in Buffalo and threw down a 1:03.50 for the 100 meter breaststroke, did the phone start ringing off the hook. Dave made recruiting trips to Michigan, Texas and Auburn before choosing Auburn. "All of these schools had great programs but I really liked the team atmosphere at Auburn," he recalls. "Besides, Michigan had Scott Werner. At Auburn I'd be the top guy."

At the Colorado state high school championships, Denniston zipped through the 100 yard breast in 54.57 seconds, the fastest time in the nation that year and just off Nelson Diebel's national high school record of 54.35.

Dave continued to improve at Auburn, and his freshman year he took third in the NCAA 100 yard breaststroke in 53.65 as Auburn placed second to Stanford.

In 1999, Auburn and Stanford were locked in a fierce rivalry for NCAA team supremacy. Auburn had walloped Stanford in 1997 then Stanford had returned the favor, and then some, in '98. The Tigers had started the '99 meet with a roar, but by the third and final day, they were winding down and in trouble. "We were hurting," explains Auburn coach David Marsh. "That's when Dave decided to assume the burden of carrying Auburn's hopes on his own shoulders, though he was only a sophomore."

Dave adds "We were falling apart. The guys who should have been making finals were only making consols, and the guys who should have been making consols weren't finishing in the top 16. We were in big trouble."

"I had the 200 breast on Day 3. We needed a big performance to pick up our sagging spirits. So I decided to lay it all on the line in prelims."

"It worked. I knocked almost two seconds off my personal best and qualified first in 1:56."

Marsh says, "That turned things around for us. The team got really psyched after watching Dave's swim and we finished the morning on a high note. I was really touched that Dave risked sacrificing himself for the sake of the team."

Almost right. Actually, though his extraordinary prelim performance was calculated to boost the team, Dave had no thought of self sacrifice.

"Now that I had qualified first, I really wanted to win it, so I decided to use the same tactic in the finals – go out as hard as I could, then try to hang on.

"We took the top three spots in consols, and that took the pressure off me. I was actually smiling as I got up on the blocks. No one had ever seen me do that before."

Denniston took the race out very hard – 54.1 at the 100 – to build a substantial lead. At the 150, he turned ahead of Mike Barrowman's American record pace. Then the proverbial grand piano landed flat on his back.

"It really hurt, but I expected it," Dave says. "I was prepared for the pain and I could deal with it," He touched first in 1:55.51, and Auburn went on to win the team title.

The focus of the 2000 season was the Olympic Trials, but Dave managed to take second behind Ed Moses in both the 100 and 200 breast at the NCAA's.

The Trials produced mixed results. Dave was unnerved after being stranded at the hotel right before his 100 meter final and he swam poorly and finished fifth. However his protégé at Auburn, Pat Calhoun, had the race of his life and made the team, finishing second to Moses.

"Though disappointed in his own performance, Dave was genuinely happy for Pat," recalls Coach Marsh. "That really showed his character."

"It was tough going back to Auburn for my senior year," Dave says. "But after a few months I got it together." The result was two personal bests at the NCAA's, both behind Texas' Brendan Hansen – 52.62 for the 100 and 1:53.48 for the 200. It was a great way to end his college career.

"After that swim, Rowdy Gaines talked to me and convinced me to keep going through 2004. He suggested I contact Coach Dave Salo out in Irvine, California. I did, and soon I was back in the water in Irvine with only one thing on my mind, the 2004 Olympic Games."

Now, if this story were to follow the script of one of those two minute "Up Close" vignettes, Dave's plucky decision to keep on training after his disappointment in 2000 would be rewarded with a berth on the 2004 U.S. Olympic team. But that's not the way it happened.

Oh, coming into 2004, things looked good. Dave made the U.S. teams for the 2002 Pan Pacific Championships and the 2003 World Championships. But in 2004, Dave's story took the more usual less chronicled turn. The kind NBC doesn't tell you about. Though he swam strongly at the Olympic Trials, Dave wound up fourth in the 100 and sixth in the 200.

This time, Dave acknowledged his competitive career was over. He remained at NOVA, coaching the 8 & under group, as he mulled over his options, including an age group coaching offer in New Zealand. He was excited by the possibility and planned to fly to Auckland in March to check it out.

Before he left Dave decided to spend a few days, as he had so often in the past, at the family cabin, 10,000 feet high in Wyoming's Snowy Range.

"The cabin's been in the family for more than 50 years," Dave explains. "I went up with my childhood friend, Andy Miller. Dragging my 10 year old, $5.95, Walmart special Tupperware sled, we snowshoed to the cabin over eight feet of snow."

"The next morning, February 6, 2005 was Super Bowl Sunday. Andy cooked up some pancakes as we debated whether to go ice fishing or sledding. We couldn't figure out how to dig down to the ice to go fishing, so sledding it was."

"On our eighth run, I was going down a hill, head first, at maybe 40 miles per hour. All of a sudden I hit a rock, and found myself headed straight into a clump of trees, head-first. I had to react quickly, so I baled and slid. Right before hitting a tree I curled into a ball and struck it with my back."

"I thought the impact had just knocked the wind out of me. I remember Andy asking if I was okay. Then I started coughing up blood and realized I couldn't feel my legs. I yelled 'Help'! Andy ran for help."

"Meanwhile, alone for 70 minutes, I thought I was bleeding internally and was scared to death. I took the camera and recorded a video for my parents. 'Mom, Dad, I love you,' I said. And I prayed."

Meanwhile, Andy remembered there was one spot in the mountains where you could get cell phone reception. He raced to Cell Phone Rock and called 911. Forty minutes later, EMTs arrived on snowmobiles. "It was only two or three miles, but that was the most painful ride of my life," recalls Dave.

The EMTs took Dave to a hospital in Laramie, where a CAT scan revealed he had broken T10 and T11 in his back and was paralyzed from the waist down. The devastating news could have been worse – there was no internal bleeding.

The hospital in Laramie was not equipped to conduct the surgery Dave required and it was too foggy for a helicopter. So Dave was taken by ambulance to the Poudre Valley Hospital in Fort Collins, Colorado. Though he was on a morphine drip, the ride was still very painful.

The surgery was scheduled for the next day. Dave called his parents in New Mexico and they called Dave's ex-girlfriend, Jessamyn Miller, with whom he had remained close.

By the time Dave went under, his mom and dad and Jessamyn were on their way to Fort Collins, and they were at his side when he awoke. Shortly thereafter, his coaches Dave Marsh and Dave Salo arrived. Meanwhile, the word went out to the greater swimming community via SwimInfo.com, and more than 3,000 e-mails came pouring in from around the U.S. and, indeed, the world.

The next day, Dave was awake and joking. "The doctors say I have a 50-50 chance of ever walking again. In other words, I've got a much better chance of walking than making the 2008 Olympic Team."

"When they told me my chances were 50-50, I felt good. I saw the glass as half full. In fact, from the moment I hit the tree, my attitude changed 180 degrees. My focus became what I could do, not what I couldn't do."

"Don't get me wrong," he says. "Breaking your back sucks. But it's better to have a great attitude and a paralyzed body than a great body and a paralyzed attitude."

After beginning rehab in a Denver hospital, Dave was admitted to Project Walk in Carlsbad, California where he shares an apartment with former Auburn teammate Justin Caron. He is totally independent and is making incredible progress in rehab - recently he took 76 steps with the aid of a walker.

Meanwhile, Dave has become a sought after and, by all accounts, brilliant motivational speaker. He is writing for Swimming World, has made a host of new friends and his social calendar is booked solid.

Dave will never make the U.S. Olympic team, though he's considering swimming in Paralympic competition. You won't see a vignette about him in 2008. That's a shame. The challenges he is facing, and the inspiration he provides for others, are tributes to his Olympian spirit.

Dave was photographed on November 5, 2005 during a community swim-a-thon in La Jolla, California.

Profile contributed by Phil Whitten.

Jeff Keith

Although he lost a leg to bone cancer at age 12, Jeff Keith did not miss a stride. Literally.

Six weeks after his right leg was amputated above the knee, the athletic Fairfield, Connecticut boy who loved swimming in Long Island Sound and playing hockey, football and baseball went skiing with his parents.

During his high school years, he was captain of his school ski team and played on the lacrosse team, using a prosthetic leg.

"I vowed to myself I'd stay in sports," said Keith. "There was a two year period of chemotherapy which was not easy. But it made me a lot tougher."

Keith's life long best friend Matt Vossler remembers him being the "superstar" on their Pop Warner football team before the cancer set in. (Vossler, who still talks to Keith almost every day, remembers, "We were the only two on the team who were also taking cotillion classes.")

"One year he was perfectly healthy, and then the next year he had lost a leg," said Vossler, who now works as an executive recruiter in Darien, Connecticut. It was hard for other youngsters to deal with Keith's illness. "I think people were a little frightened by it, how come that guy doesn't have one leg, how come he doesn't have any hair. I can only imagine how tough it was for Jeff with the hair loss and all of those other issues at age 12 and 13."

But Keith didn't let it get him down, and his brother Dave and close friends didn't either.

"We never let him feel sorry for himself," Vossler said.

Vossler and Keith both went on to Boston College and were roommates there. Keith continued to make his mark as an athlete, playing goalie on the varsity lacrosse team, swimming his senior year and competing in triathlons.

Then after graduating from college in 1984, Keith got the wacky idea of running across the country.

With the help of his brother, Vossler, and three other college friends, along with support from several non-profit foundations, Keith set about organizing a cross-country run to raise money for cancer research.

And at the age of 22, he ran across the country.

He averaged 16 miles a day for eight months until he covered the more than 3,000 miles. He started in Boston and jogged through cities including St. Louis, Missouri; Vincennes, Indiana; Magnolina, New Mexico and Tempe, Arizona on his way to Marina del Rey, California, where he ran right into the ocean.

Along the way he raised funds and stopped in hospitals to talk with cancer patients and survivors. He fueled himself by eating pasta five days a week along with fruits and vegetables, Powerade and one daily beer. His support crew drove with him in a Winnebago, which is where he slept most nights. "It became very crowded by the end, but my road crew and I had a great bonding experience," he said.

The trip made Keith the first and still the only amputee to run across the country. Only 80 some runners have made the trek.

Dave Keith, who works as a painter in Bridgeport, Connecticut, said the run was "an amazing thing to be part of."

"It's something I think about every day of my life," said Dave, who is older than Jeff by two years. "It brings tears to my eyes. What can I say, he's my idol."

After the run Keith headed off to get his MBA at the University of Southern California, but he stayed close with Vossler and other supporters in Connecticut.

He had had enough of running.

But he hadn't had enough of fundraising, awareness raising and serving as an inspiration. And he hadn't had enough of endurance sports. Vossler and other friends old and new were also interested in starting another fundraising endeavor. So they turned their focus to swimming.

"We decided to do something not unlike Jeff's run," said Vossler, who, inspired by Keith, had started doing triathlons. "We didn't want to do your standard 10K or golf tournament (to raise money)."

So in 1987 while Keith was still at USC, he and Vossler co-founded Swim Across the Sound, a race across Long Island Sound to raise money for cancer research. After he got his MBA, Keith moved back to Connecticut and began swimming again in Long Island Sound for fun and training.

In 1991 he and Vossler left the Swim Across the Sound organization and started a new one called Swim Across America (SAA). Their first event was a 26 mile relay crossing of Nantucket Sound from Nantucket to Hyannis on Cape Cod.

More events were added to the SAA calendar over the years, including a race down the Hudson River, an annual event in Lake Michigan off Chicago and a swim at

Nantasket Beach in Boston. The Nantucket swim was discontinued in the mid 1990's because it had become such a logistical challenge. Extremely variable weather conditions and rough waters made it a gamble whether the swim would even take place each year.

Keith still counts the Nantucket swim as one of the more difficult he has ever done. "The water is incredibly rough and the currents are unpredictable at times," he said. After four or five miles during the 1992 Nantucket Swim, he tagged it "probably the hardest body of water I ever encountered."

But he calls his 10.5 mile solo swim on Candlewood Lake in Danbury, Connecticut in 2003 his toughest swim ever. "It's fresh water and there is no buoyancy as in salt water, so you have to have a good kick to stay up on top of the water for that long."

To date, Swim Across America has raised more than $10 million for cancer research, prevention and treatment and helped more than 18,000 cancer patients and their families, according to its website. Research beneficiaries include the Dana-Farber Cancer Institute in Boston, Memorial Sloan-Kettering Cancer Center in New York, the Children's Hospital of New York and the Cardinal Bernardin Cancer Institute in Chicago.

At one of the Swim Across America events Keith met a backstroker named Karin Andren, who was training for the 1988 Olympic Trials at the time. Andren, captain of the University of North Carolina Tar Heels squad in 1991, "trained me," Keith said. The two hit it off, and in 1995 they were married.

Today Keith continues to participate in Swim Across America every year, but leaves most of the organizational aspects to staff and over 1,000 volunteers. The organization brings together grassroots volunteers and participants with Olympians including Steve Lundquist, Craig Beardsley, Jenny Thompson, Theresa Andrews, Rowdy Gaines and Janel Jorgensen, who now serves as executive director of SAA.

"It's become a mature event. It's taken on a life of its own and kind of runs itself now," Keith said.

So Keith took the skills he learned from SAA to launch another similar project, this time with biking, called the Connecticut Challenge. The Connecticut Challenge held its inaugural race on August 27-28, 2005. The event featured 25, 50 and 100 mile rides and various kinds of festivities. Keith plans to expand the organization to include a variety of other bike events.

He said his target for 2007 is to raise $750,000 with all the proceeds designated to fund the "Connecticut Challenge Adult Survivorship Clinic" at the Yale Cancer Center, named in honor of the bike event. Among other things the center addresses the long-term consequences of childhood and adult cancer treatments like heart problems, fertility issues, lymphedema, post traumatic stress, impaired growth, osteoporosis and increased risk of second cancers.

"Cancer survivors will be screened for these complications and learn how to minimize or avoid future problems," Keith said. "Patients can see a variety of specialists in one day. The clinic will also offer psychosocial support to those whose lives have been forever changed by cancer."

Today, Jeff and Karin Keith live in Fairfield, Connecticut and have three kids. Keith juggles fatherhood and running Connecticut Challenge with his job as a high yield bond salesman at UBS. And he still manages to train five days a week, alternating biking and swimming in Long Island Sound and also doing Pilates and yoga. He has a prosthetic specially designed for biking and an innovative "C-leg" with a computer chip in the knee.

Vossler, who serves on the board of the Connecticut Challenge, said he believes there are two main aims in the organizations. They both raise awareness of and resources for cancer prevention and survivors, and foster a spirit of inspiration and determination in general.

"Every day you come across people who are battling cancer," he noted. "It's something that's part of our lives. It's about helping people know they can overcome challenges and adversity in their lives. Whether you're cycling 100 miles or having another dose of chemo or just having a bad day, it's amazing to realize the amount of strength and confidence you can get."

Throughout his "triathlon" of fundraising events – the cross country run, SAA and Connecticut Challenge – Keith feels he has provided motivation and hope to many cancer patients and survivors. He noted that one young man who participated in the bike event was inspired to run from San Francisco to Boston.

"I think organizations like Swim Across America and Connecticut Challenge can inspire others to do great things," Keith said. "About once a month I get a cancer related phone call. Last week a 15 year old boy called who was getting his leg amputated and wanted to talk to me before it happened. It's very rewarding for me to be able to talk to these folks. The message we want to get across to people is that you can in fact make a difference."

Jeff was photographed September 11, 2005 on Sasco Beach in Fairfield, Connecticut. Profile contributed by Kari Lydersen.

Dawn Blue Gerken

Dawn Blue Gerken knew that her body was not healthy in the fall of 1986. The tip-off wasn't just the rashes, the swollen joints and the persistent tiredness that plagued the then 12 year old from Lakewood, Ohio. "I kind of figured it out from the skull and cross-bones on the IV bag," Dawn, now 32 and the head coach of the men's and women's swim and diving teams at Massachusetts Institute of Technology, says about her first chemotherapy session. "I was like, 'Oh, this must be a bad thing.'"

It was a very bad thing. Dawn, already a promising swimmer, was starting seventh grade when she was diagnosed with lupus, an autoimmune disorder that causes the body to create antibodies that attack its organs. About 16,000 Americans develop lupus every year, but Dawn's case was particularly severe. Doctors said that her kidney was in danger of shutting down and prescribed experimental chemotherapy treatments to fight the disease.

So instead of attending swim practices and hanging out with friends in the fall of 1986, Dawn took chemotherapy sessions once a month for six months. She would start those days with six hours of preparatory fluids, and then she'd receive the chemo for 90 minutes. She'd spend the rest of the weekend vomiting and nauseous. Then she would take Monday off from school and be back in class on Tuesday, "hiding everything," she says. "It was a pretty lonely and depressed couple years there."

Fortunately, the chemotherapy worked on the lupus. After six months she was able to swim again and go back to school full time. Within two years she was temporarily off all medicine. Still, the steroids that Dawn took as part of her treatment had affected her body. The athletic, 85 pound girl who started seventh grade in the fall was transformed into a 130 pound "monster," as Dawn described herself. Swimming worked best to counteract her own insecurity about her new body and the cruel comments of other teenagers.

"I remember the first practices were pretty tough. With a different body and with losing all that strength, I was pretty slow and pretty out of shape. But I kept going back every day, and I wasn't embarrassed to be in a swimming suit."

"Swimming played a huge part in making me feel normal. I looked forward to practices and I think it was at that point that I really changed my attitude toward swimming. It wasn't something that I dreaded, it was something that I got to do. I wasn't allowed to do it for so long, and then I was allowed to go back to swim practice and I tried to make the most of it. I got good. All of a sudden I was good."

Twenty years later, Dawn is in her fourth season coaching the MIT swimming teams. She is one of the few female coaches in the country to lead both the men's and women's teams. Her rise in the college coaching ranks followed a stellar collegiate swimming career. Dawn was a seven-time All-American breaststroker at Smith College and was named the New England Swimmer of the Year in 1996.

But before Dawn dominated the pool at Smith, she had to struggle through high school with her lupus symptoms. Although she returned to swimming in the seventh grade, Dawn had to stay out of the sun because sun might stimulate a relapse. In the summer she trained outdoors, but before the sun rose. In eighth grade her hard work began to pay off. That summer she made the Lake Erie Zone Team, made up of the top 13 to 14 year old swimmers in the region.

When she was in high school the training increased, and Dawn regularly logged 10,000 yards a day. In tenth grade her family moved and Dawn started at a new high school, but her swimming successes continued. Breaking school records along the way, she made the Ohio State swim meet that year. Unfortunately, Dawn had a relapse in eleventh grade. She says it was because she was going through a rebellious period and went out in the sun, which caused her symptoms to flare up. Dawn went back onto chemotherapy treatment but still swam. Following high school Dawn knew that she wanted to continue swimming competitively, and she found her niche at Smith, where she still holds the Smith College records in both the 100 and 200 yard breaststroke, with times of 1:06.92 and 2:23.95, respectively.

Part of the reason that Dawn became a swimming coach shortly after college was to make up for the last meet of her college career, one of her lowest competitive moments. This was in 1996, the year she was named the New England Swimmer of the Year, when Dawn set two meet records at the New England regional competition, the qualifier for the NCAA Nationals.

"I came out of this having all these expectations that I had heaped on myself. I really wanted to win Nationals, I thought that would be a good way for me to end, and that I would be OK with my career ending that way."

Instead, as one of the favorites in the 100 yard breaststroke, Dawn tightened up, placed ninth and failed to qualify for the final heat. In the 200 yard event the next day she was still so upset that she considered pulling out. Instead she swam poorly and didn't crack

the top 16. It was Dawn's first true taste of swimming failure.

"I was just devastated after that. I think that so much about me being OK with myself and having self confidence was tied into my swimming. It wasn't just about me not swimming well, it was about all those years of being sick and being un-normal and affected. That really came out after that last race where I didn't perform. All of a sudden I wasn't healthy, normal Dawn. I was sick Dawn again. I cried for a day after that. I don't think it was about the 200 breaststroke. It was about acceptance of myself."

But swimming stayed a constant for Dawn following college. She coached age group swimmers for three years before returning to school for a Masters degree in Exercise and Sports Studies, a program that trains students to become head coaches. Dawn broke into the coaching ranks at Vassar in 2001, where she was the assistant coach for one year and then the interim head coach the following year. In 2003 the head coach position at MIT opened up. The position was especially appealing because the school had just completed a new swimming facility. "When I applied I didn't think I had a chance because I knew that a lot of people wanted to be there," Dawn says. Luckily, she was wrong.

Today Dawn lives in Cambridge, Massachusetts, near the MIT campus. She still meets two times a year with doctors to monitor her lupus. The only obvious remaining effect from the lupus is that Dawn has to be very careful about going out in the sun. "Most people that I meet have no idea that I have a chronic illness, and they are very surprised when they find out."

The MIT swim teams have been highly successful under Dawn. She says that her coaching style is a combination of "intensity" and "keeping it light," and so far her teams have responded well. The 2005 men's team finished tenth in the nation in Division III, and the 2006 women's team finished twentieth nationally. Since the fall of 2003 the two teams have combined to break thirty MIT swimming records, three quarters of the records the school holds. Dawn says that she likes coaching at a place where "they swim because they really love it, not because they are on athletic scholarships." Academics always come first, she says.

One of Dawn's favorite aspects of coaching is the teamwork that she sees among her students. "I love to win. I love the whole thrill of racing. But more than the performance, my favorite aspect of competitive swimming is the friendship, the camaraderie, and this is one of the things that I stress with my team. I want to win Conferences, and I want to win Nationals, but more importantly it's the family that we have."

Dawn was photographed on November 5, 2004 in Boston, Massachusetts.
Profile contributed by Jeremy Shweder.

WHITE

Noah White

When Noah White contacted the swim coach of the Naval Academy after his junior year of high school to ask if he could swim on the team, he got back a note saying, essentially, "Thanks, but no thanks."

"He wrote that the Academy is a great academic opportunity and things like that, but they were only looking to recruit swimmers with Junior National cuts (qualifying standards)," says White, a native of El Cajon in Southern California, who had been swimming with his local club team since age five.

But with his quick laugh, easy going manner and quiet sense of determination, White was never one to be discouraged.

"I was just sure I wanted to go to Navy," he remembers. "It sounded like such a great adventure." So despite the disheartening reception from the coach, Noah decided on the Academy anyway.

He met, then Navy coach, Lee "Lou" Lawrence in person during an intense summer program for incoming students before entering as a freshman and again didn't receive much encouragement. All the participants were required to do sports during the boot camp week, and White was drawn to basketball because he was intimidated by the high caliber of the swimming recruits at the school. But entering his "plebe" year in the fall he joined the swim team nonetheless.

"They would cut swimmers, so my whole first two years I was always dreading being cut," says White, who had moderate success at local high school and club meets in the San Diego area but had never really stood out in the swimming world. "But I guess they saw something in me, because they kept me around."

He didn't do a single best time during his first year, and he says he got last or second to last in most races.

"As a plebe they make you do all these difficult things, like you always have to run down the passageways between buildings and classes and turn the corners sharply shouting 'Go Navy, Beat Army,' it's called chopping," he says. "Things that swimmers at other schools don't need to deal with just to get to the pool. You're just exhausted all the time."

Bill Roberts, who became Navy's head men's coach after Lawrence retired, agreed that the extra hazing can take a toll on some athletes.

"Some kids will really struggle with plebe year before they adjust. Handling that level of stress does have an effect," he says. "But indirectly the Navy's doing some great extra coaching for us. They're gaining strength they didn't have, and that translates into the water sometimes. Every year some freshmen really take off and some freshmen plateau."

Going into his junior year at Navy in Annapolis, however, White felt something had changed. For one thing he had grown from a scrawny 6'4" and 150 pounds to 6'7" and 190 pounds. Also, he had been inspired by reading the book "Gold in the Water": The True Story of Ordinary Men and their Extraordinary Dream of Olympic Glory by swimmer and journalist P.H. Mullen, chronicling the efforts of two Santa Clara Swim Club men aiming toward the Olympics in 2000.

"I was pumped up to swim, I was training more than ever before," he says.

He was excited going into the first meets that season, but his optimism didn't bear immediate results.

"The first meet I still got last, and the one after that too!" he remembers.

Up until that point he had been specializing in backstroke.

"They let me do the 100 free in a relay my freshman year and I went a few seconds slower than they expected and I lost it for them, so it was a while before they let me do the 100 free again!" he laughed.

But since he had been sprinting well in workout, during his junior year the coaches decided to give him another shot. And they were immediately impressed.

"It was at an Army-Navy meet before Christmas, which is always the big one, and they were a body length ahead," he says. "I caught up and went two or three seconds better than my best PR (personal record)."

By the end of that year, he was breaking school records.

Things had just really come together: his growth spurt, his increasing confidence and motivation and the fact that he had finally found his stride as far as the academic and physical demands of the Academy.

When Lawrence retired, with three decades at Navy under his belt, at the farewell celebration White publicly presented him with the "thanks but no thanks" letter.

"Everyone was cracking up," White says.

Roberts, the new head coach, recalled how White came into his office and proclaimed that he could be the best sprinter on the team even though Navy was rich in sprint talent that year. He took the young man's word for it and decided to move White to the sprint group with coach Patrick "McGee" Moody.

"His junior year was his breakout year," says Roberts. "When I asked McGee what are you going to do with Noah, he looked at me like I had two heads. Noah had always trained with the distance swimmers."

But the move worked, and White just kept getting faster, ending up with the school record in the 100 free and the sixth fastest 50 time in Navy history. At the Patriot League championships, he won the 50, 100 and 200 free and was on four winning relays including Navy's winning 400 free relay, which he anchored, at the very end of the meet. "We almost never won that relay, it was usually Harvard or Princeton," he says. "When I dove in with all the guys along the side chanting 'Noah, Noah…' There was nothing like it."

He also made automatic NCAA qualifying standards, no small feat. At the NCAA's he placed 31st in the 50 free, 29th in the 100 and 43rd in the 200 free.

He was also succeeding in the classroom, where he graduated in the class of 2004 with a 3.27 GPA in systems engineering, and was named the Patriot League Male Scholar Athlete of the Year.

The summer following graduation, White swam in a series of high profile meets attempting to make the qualifying cuts for the Olympic Trials. He ended up qualifying for both the 50 and 100 free, the 50 cut swimming alone in a time trial at 8pm after he'd narrowly missed it during his race.

At Trials he was slower than his best times, having tapered and shaved for three consecutive meets leading up to the Trials in order to make his cuts. ("Tapering and shaving" is when a swimmer reduces their training load to get their muscles rested and primed for the big race, and shaves off most of their body hair to reduce drag in the water.)

"It was tough getting ready for all those high stakes meets in a row," he says. "I was in good shape, but not in good racing shape."

Yet he was thrilled nonetheless with his experience throughout the summer at Trials and after.

"I was swimming next to Ian Crocker and Gary Hall Jr.," he says, referring to some of the most famous sprinters in the sport. "At the Janet Evans Invitational (in southern California before Olympic Trials) I was warming up and I look over and (Australian legend) Ian Thorpe is right next to me. It's exciting to swim next to those people you always read about, even if you can't beat them! It takes being at the very bottom to really appreciate that."

White laughs at the memory of making the front page of a Long Beach newspaper for reasons other than he would have hoped during Trials. The paper did a feature on people who came in last in first heats at the meet.

"But I was happy just to be there," he says. "If you had told anyone two years ago that I would be at Olympic Trials, they would just have laughed."

What kept him going during those early years? Did he just love the sport so much that he didn't mind coming in last again and again?

"I hated the first two years (at Navy)!" he admits. "There's nothing fun about trying your hardest and going through all the other stuff at the Academy too and then going to a meet and getting last every time. What keeps you going is your teammates, being part of a team. Now I realize that the reason I did so well my senior year is that I persevered through all of that."

And he never thought of quitting?

"As an athlete, being a quitter just isn't high up there on your list of desirable moral attributes," he said. "Especially in the military culture."

After Olympic Trials, White hung his suit up and headed on to another challenge – learning to man a Navy nuclear submarine. That means U.S. Navy Nuclear Power School in Charleston, South Carolina where he spends 12 hour days learning, among other things, about the nuclear systems that power submarines. After school he will be on subs for deployments of around six months. Not an easy task mentally or physically for any-one, and in a specialty that tends to select for shorter guys, White's height will make it even more challenging. Did the training and focus necessary for swimming help prepare him for such a stressful career? Even over the phone you can hear the shrug in his voice. White is taking on this phase of his life with the same nonchalant modesty that charac-terized his swimming success.

"I think swimming really developed my drive to excel," he says. "The long hours of training and sticking with a job. You realize nothing's that bad compared to a sprint lac-tate set" – referring to a grueling workout where you push your body to its absolute limit, trying to reach the maximum amount of exercise induced lactic acid that your muscles can produce.

Since graduation he has gotten in the water a few times for fun, but the Navy doesn't leave much time for swimming or any other hobbies or activities. White admits that he does miss it.

"It's kind of sad looking back," he says. "That's the most fun I've had in my life."

Noah was photographed November 14, 2005 at the U.S. Naval Academy in Annapolis, Maryland.

Profile contributed by Kari Lydersen.

Mike Nyeholt

His future, much like his present, was stacked with potential. He was a good looking man, intelligent and the owner of a go-get-'em work ethic. He was a phenomenal athlete: a nationally ranked swimmer in the middle distance disciplines. He was adventurous, typically in search of an activity that would get the blood flowing. Mike Nyeholt, a Southern California boy to the max, had the world at his disposal.

Temporarily, though, the future that seemed his for the taking was lost during an early January day in 1981. Nyeholt, who had fondness for dirt bike riding, sometimes along the Colorado River, was enjoying a motorcycle excursion in Blythe on the California-Arizona border with his then girlfriend. Nyeholt's outing went smoothly during the early portion of his trek. Then, suddenly, his life changed.

When the front wheel of Nyeholt's bike hit a bump, the front end of his vehicle dug into the ground and propelled Mike into the air and over his handlebars. Wearing a helmet, Nyeholt thought quickly while airborne and made an effort to tuck and roll upon impact. However, when he hit the ground, Mike's neck couldn't withstand the pressure and he suffered compression fractures to his C-7 and T-1 vertebrae.

Conscious, but motionless and sprawled on the desert floor, Nyeholt knew something was wrong as he waited for medical attention. He couldn't move. He couldn't feel. But little did he know, his misfortune – eventually – would turn into a positive development, in the form of the University of Southern California Physically Challenged Athletes Scholarship Fund.

Today, Nyeholt is a highly successful businessman and hardly limited by the accident that left him relearning to walk, albeit with the aid of crutches. A relationship manager with the Capital Guardian Trust Company, Nyeholt handles client servicing for large public pension plans. In his job, he travels approximately 65 percent of the time, not easy for a man whose crash left him paralyzed from the chest down. Yet, as successful as Nyeholt has become in the business world, his relationship with "Swim With Mike" can be viewed as his greatest achievement.

Following the dirt bike accident, Nyeholt spent months building up strength and movement in his limbs. He regained the use of his arms fairly quickly then gradually enhanced the strength in his lower body during a two to three month rehabilitation. A toe wiggle was followed by the flexing of his ankle, which was followed by the lifting of his legs. Slowly, but with determination and a positive mindset, Nyeholt pushed forward. In time, he was navigating with a walker and crutches. These days, Mike uses a wheelchair around the office or on arduous days. However, he prefers walking when he's at his Pasadena, California home.

Not surprisingly, the days and months following the accident were difficult for Nyeholt. Coming out of high school, he had been recruited by coach Peter Daland to swim for USC. By the time his collegiate career (1974-78) came to a close, he was a member of three NCAA championship teams and had finished ninth in the 400 meter freestyle at the 1976 United States Olympic Trials. Nyeholt, simply, was one of the nation's elite swimmers.

When, a few years later, he was forced to adjust to a vastly different lifestyle, he spent four to five years asking himself the typical question of an individual dealt a poor hand. Why me? He also went through a period in which he took his frustration out on his family and friends. Despite his difficult moments, Nyeholt was surrounded by an unbreakable support system, one that led to the creation of the awe inspiring fundraiser Swim With Mike.

In the spring of 1981, Mike's friends began brainstorming ways to raise money for a specially equipped van that would allow Nyeholt to maneuver around Southern California. Ultimately, Ron Orr and Mike's other pals decided on a swim-a-thon to be held at the Industry Hills Aquatic Club. Those attending would swim laps and donate the collected funds to benefit Nyeholt.

Mike, who was not yet out of the hospital, was determined to attend the event in his name. So, wearing a halo and in traction, Nyeholt appeared at the first "Swim For Mike", the original name of the affair. He was so blown away by the event that he made a promise that he would take part a year later. True to his word, Nyeholt indeed was in the water when the second gathering was held. It had been renamed "Swim With Mike", the name it still carries. That second year, Nyeholt was inspired to dazzle and cranked out a body-beating 200 lengths of the pool. When the first year of the swimathon raised more money than necessary to purchase Nyeholt's van, the remaining funds went toward a scholarship fund for physically challenged athletes.

A quarter century has passed since that initial fundraiser, and more than $5.5 million has been raised and put toward 54 full scholarships for USC students who have overcome their own physical limitations. The event is now held at the McDonald's Swim

Stadium on the campus of USC and Nyeholt has become co-chair of the "Swim With Mike" organizing committee.

During the term of the fundraiser, many of the original faces have remained, and a number of celebrities have stopped by, including former president Gerald Ford, actress Betty White, and Rafer Johnson, the 1960 Olympic gold medalist in the decathlon. Orr, one of the originators of the fundraiser, is currently USC's Associate Athletic Director. And Nyeholt's former college teammates, Olympians John Naber and Bruce Furniss, have played major roles in the development of the swim-a-thon.

There was a time when Mike Nyeholt was staring at a future with a stacked upside. Well, the man has certainly met those lofty expectations, although not according to the original blueprint. Instead, Nyeholt has proven that a devastating injury does not spell the end, but can spark a new beginning. He has dealt with paralysis and has used a strong will and upbeat outlook to establish himself as a prominent businessman. And from his potential tragedy has come not only benefit for himself, but also for others.

Unquestionably, the Mike Nyeholt Story is a triumphant tale.

Mike was photographed August 2, 2005 in his office in Los Angeles, California.
Profile contributed by John Lohn.

Marcella MacDonald, D.P.M.

After Marcella MacDonald finished her first crossing of the English Channel on June 30, 1994 having survived 10 hours and 33 minutes in frigid water and bumpy waves to swim 21 miles from England to France, her younger sister congratulated her on fulfilling a childhood promise.

Maybe it was just the brain freeze, but Marcella was confused.

She didn't remember having said anything about the English Channel as a child. She had gotten the bug to do the swim when she was studying medicine in New York City and when she met another channel swimmer in Connecticut. But her sister Teresa, seven years her junior, remembers that when Marcella was about 12 years old, she vowed that she would both swim the English Channel and become a doctor.

Now Marcella, a podiatrist practicing in her native Manchester, Connecticut, has accomplished both.

"Maybe there is destiny!" she says.

Swimming the English Channel once would be a feat for anyone. But it was just the beginning for Marcella. The day after her first crossing, on the harbor beach in Dover, England where channel swimmers often train, she met Freda Streeter, mother of legendary Channel swimmer Alison Streeter, who is now a London currency trader and member of Marcella's boat crew.

"She has intuition about swimmers," Marcella says of Freda. "She congratulated me on my time, then asked when I was coming back for a double. She planted the seed. I kind of laughed it off, but as the year went on and no one was attempting it, I started thinking about it. It wasn't an obsession, but it was a passion, a goal for me."

She made her first attempt at a double crossing in July 1997, but tore her right triceps in the choppy waves during the first few hours and had to stop after a single 12 hour 57 minute crossing.

"It happened in the third hour," she says. "By the fifth hour I knew I wasn't heading back. I was just in excruciating pain every stroke. I was glad I made it across."

It took her six months to recover from the injury, but gradually she got back to training. Then on her next double crossing attempt, in August 1999, a maritime accident the night before about 30 miles north of the swim route doomed her chances. In the morning, an oil tanker was still burning and tons of waste had been dumped into the water.

"I don't know what I was breathing in, but I've never felt so sick in my life," Marcella says. "Some of my crew got sick, everything I took in I was throwing up."

In August 2000 she tried yet again, but after a single nine hour, 42 minute crossing to France, she succumbed to the cold in the 14th hour and climbed the ladder onto her escort boat, the "Aegean Blue."

These three solo crossings would be major achievements for anyone. But Marcella was still driven to make the double. Once she sets her mind to something, she says, she wants to accomplish it. And she knew she had a double crossing in her.

So finally on July 27-28, 2001 she did it. After 21 hours and 19 minutes in 62 degree water, she clambered onto the slippery rocks of Abbott's Cove and at age 37 became the first American woman and seventh woman worldwide to do a double crossing.

"I felt like someone beat me up with a baseball bat at the end," she says. "That's the only way I can describe it. That was my fourth try, so I was just very happy and relieved that it was over with."

Since then she has completed another double crossing and another single one, bringing her total number of crossings to eight, the most for any American woman. Less than two weeks after her July 6, 2003 solo crossing, she also participated in a double crossing relay in which swimmers alternate swimming for one hour each.

But she still hadn't had enough.

On September 3-4, 2004 Marcella tried for a mind-and-body numbing triple crossing. After making a double crossing in 23 hours, she stopped one hour later because of shoulder pain.

Marcella's partner of 11 years, Janet Galya, was in her boat crew. She has "watched every stroke I have done," as Marcella says, in every crossing except the first one. Having Janet in the boat cheering her on gives Marcella invaluable moral support, she says.

One of seven children, Marcella's swimming career is something of a family affair. On her first crossing her parents John and Teresa and her sister Joanne were on the boat along with her brother Ken, who served as crew chief. During her 1997 and 1999 swims her twin sister Beth, also a swimmer, was on the boat. Janet now serves as crew chief, working closely with her regular boat captain, Mike Oram, one of the sport's legendary Channel crossing guides.

"They know how I swim, when to feed me, when to ignore my whining and when to believe me and get me out of the water," she says.

After her 2004 crossing Marcella took a "break" from the channel to do other open water swims. But she still can't get the channel out of her mind.

"I still wake up every morning with the white cliffs and blue channel water in my mind," she says.

Marcella does most of her training – 40,000 to 50,000 yards a week – in the pool. She also does open water training at Hammonasett State Park in Connecticut with some of her channel-swimming friends. During periods of heavy training, she gets up at 4:30am to swim for two or three hours before her office hours begin at 9:30am, and she usually spends her lunch hours at a local gym for dryland work. Along with this training and her podiatry practice, she also finds time to coach the 8 and under novice group of the Laurel East Hartford YMCA swim team two days a week.

"I love to talk to the older swimmers about goals and challenges and doing their best," she says. "With the little ones I teach stroke mechanics and to always have fun."

Like many ultra endurance athletes, Marcella often gets asked the question "Why?"

"Life is too short, that's one of the reasons I do the things I do," she said. "I believe I was given a gift to swim long distances in cold water, and I'm going to keep doing it until I don't feel the need to do it anymore."

The English Channel almost never gets above 65 degrees Fahrenheit even on a hot summer day, usually it is in the low 60's. To qualify for her first crossing, Marcella did a 10 hour swim in 60 degree water in New Hampshire's Lake Sunapee.

Over the years she has also done a number of other marathon swims including the Swim Across the Sound, a 17 mile race across Long Island Sound to raise money for St. Vincent's Medical Center Foundation, and the 28.5 mile Manhattan Island marathon race in which swimmers circle New York city.

Contrary to some stereotypes, successful Channel swimmers are not swaddled in huge rolls of fat, rather it is a matter of balancing body fat for warmth with muscle and some degree of sleekness. At 5'8" and a muscular 180 pounds, Marcella feels she is now at her ideal weight. During her 2003 crossing she was about 10 pounds lighter, and although she felt great on land, she suffered in the water.

"I was cold," she says. "I got this spastic shivering of the thighs."

On her 2004 crossing she was about eight pounds heavier than now, probably more weight than she needed. "It's a balance because you have to pull the extra weight," she notes. "I'm going for a happy medium."

She feels part of her Channel success is the result of years of swimming in the pool as an age grouper and on the Manchester High School team. "It's definitely easier for me than someone who wasn't a swimmer growing up," says Marcella, who also played softball in high school. "I grew up training, and I always had the mentality of being a good practice swimmer. I never had fast twitch muscles, I learned to accept distance swimming. So when I did the first crossing it hit me, I really belong here!"

And what does she think about all that time in the water?

"I really do concentrate on my swim," she says. "I do things you could call accounting. I count my stroke cycles. Then when I really start hurting I start praying. I do many cycles of the rosary, that keeps me in a zone. You have to take it a half hour at a time. If you start thinking you have 10 more hours to go, you'd go crazy and get out. You have to not worry about it and think eventually you'll get there. I also never think about what's underneath me, or I'd hyperventilate."

She never set out to become an expert on the currents or geography of the Channel. In fact she has tried to resist learning "too much" about the place where she has spent so many excruciating hours.

"I'm learning more and more about the tides and traffic, but I'm trying not to think about it," she says. "Because then I know where I am and how much farther I have, and that drives me crazy. I want to just swim and then suddenly hear (boat captain) Mike say, 'Give me a good half hour and you'll be on the rocks.'"

Marcella reports that in the latter part of the 1990's and start of 2000, there was a "renaissance" of interest in the Channel and crossings. She credits that not only to aspiring

Channel crossers but also the logistical support structure in England, namely the Channel Swimming & Piloting Federation, which organizes boats to accompany swimmers across the treacherous waters, fills out the necessary paper work and helps monitor weather conditions.

"They're giving their day and night for the safety of these swimmers," she says of the boat pilots and crew. "It's a business for them, but they're not making a lot of money off it. Without them no one would be able to do it. They are our lifeline."

She comments that there are three main different types of channel swimmers.

"I am a very laid back swimmer. I know what I need to do and I know a lot of unexpected things will happen which you have to just let roll off your back. Then you have the swimmers who take everything very seriously. But when you're talking about open water you're talking about a non controlled setting. It's not like a pool. I tell these people just relax, have some fun! And then you have the other extreme, some people who have this pipe dream about swimming the channel. They have no idea what they're getting into. The channel is a very humbling place. That's the best way you can describe that baby. I've been with swimmers who would have smoked me in the pool, but you put me in the channel with them, and everything gets equaled out."

When Marcella first researched channel swimming in 1992, "we didn't have the internet so it wasn't easy to get information. You'd send a letter or make your long distance phone calls and think, 'Am I ever going to hear from them?'"

Now the internet hosts a lively community of Channel swimmers, she says, who are supportive and eager to share information with each other. There are 10 swimmers in Connecticut who have crossed the channel, an inordinately high number from one small state. The group gets together to swim and swap stories periodically.

"It's amazing how many people want to swim the channel," she says. "I've met so many amazing friends. I have contacts in India, Australia, England, all over the world. It's an extended family. Whether you've swam it or have a loved one who has or you're a pilot or an observer or crew member for a swimmer, we're all connected. I love to go up to Dover Castle and look across that water, and think, 'How can we swim across that?' It blows my mind."

Marcella was photographed July 5, 2005 on Hammonasset Beach in Madison, Connecticut. Profile contributed by Kari Lydersen.

Greg Bonann

Greg Bonann has received the International Swimming Hall of Fame's highest honor, the Gold Medallion Award. But you may not have heard about that.

If you enjoy armchair visits to exotic places chances are you've seen his award winning documentaries on PBS, although more than likely you didn't pay much attention to the credits at the end of the films.

Because you're reading this book, we know you are a serious swimming fan and you probably enjoy other Olympic sports as well. So you've probably seen his Olympic documentary about the 1980 Winter Games, "Fire and Ice," which won the coveted CINE Golden Eagle award. He also produced and directed stunning films about the 1984 and 1988 Olympics. But he's not George Lucas, so if you didn't catch the name when those credits were rolling, you are forgiven.

He then went on to create, sell, co-write, produce and direct what eventually became the most successful series in television history. But the guy has little desire for publicity, so there's a good chance you've never even read about him.

"He" is Greg Bonann, the creator of "Baywatch". An ex-high school and college swimmer, and current Masters swimmer, he may be the most influential former lifeguard since Ronald Reagan.

Actually, the word "former" doesn't really apply here because Greg, now in his fifties, still serves faithfully as an L.A. County beach lifeguard at Santa Monica, Temescal Canyon and Will Rogers beaches several days each year. He's been doing it since 1970.

Talk with anyone who knows Greg Bonann and, invariably, you get the same description: he is selfless, loyal, humble, generous, extremely competitive, driven, and most of all, a great friend. Every week he still swims three or four times and bikes once or twice with his bud and training partner since 1968, Bob ("BJ") Janis.

He also remains the closest of friends with his former high school swim coach, Pete Nelson. When he was to receive the Gold Medallion at an award ceremony in Fort Lauderdale he invited Nelson and his wife along, all expenses paid, and in his acceptance speech lauded the coach as the single greatest influence on his swimming career. He still spends time with Hal Dunnagin his head instructor in lifeguard school, whom he refers to fondly as "my hero." And he's had the same girlfriend, Tai Collins, for 14 years.

Greg's swimming career began inauspiciously in 1968, when he was a 10th grader at Pacific Palisades High School. He barely made the team, and was put in the distance lane, then ruled by Janis, a senior and the defending L.A. City champion in the 400 yard freestyle.

Janis recalls his first impression of the brash young man who would eventually become one of his very best friends. "He was loud, obnoxious and didn't fit in at all with the others guys in the lane, all of whom were seniors."

But Bonann, then 16, was oblivious to the initial impression he had made. Besides, he did not exactly threaten Janis' status as the number one distance guy in the pool. "I used to measure my performance by how many times he lapped me," says Bonann. "At first, he was lapping me twice in a 400, but gradually I cut down the distance between us.

"Bob was the City champion, and I think it was the day he only lapped me once that

I first realized I could become a pretty good swimmer."

Janis went on to repeat as City champion in the 400 in '68, swimming 3:52. Greg was thrilled just to make finals, recalling that Janis "didn't even lap me once in that race."

"Swimming with BJ made me a better swimmer and a better person," he says.

Greg continued to improve, finishing second at the City championships his junior year and winning the distance event when he was a senior.

After he graduated from Pali in 1970, Bonann passed the rigorous, highly competitive test to become an LA County lifeguard, and spent the summer patrolling the Temescal Canyon beach for the first time. That fall, he enrolled at Washington State University, eager to pursue his swimming career at the next level. He remained at WSU until the passage of Title IX, the federal law meant to create equality of opportunity in educational institutions for both sexes, was used as a pretext for canceling the men's swim team. So he headed south, transferring to NCAA powerhouse Long Beach State, a move he describes as pivotal.

"I was used to fill in wherever we need points," he recalls of his time at Long Beach. "I was the worst guy on a great team," he laughs. "Remember, that team featured Gunnar Larsson in the individual medley and Hans Fassnacht in the distance events, both Olympians. I wasn't ever going to beat those guys, but I was happy just to contribute."

Bonann graduated with a degree in Journalism. Unable to get into Law School, he enrolled in Business School at UCLA, receiving his MBA in 1976. There he decided to combine his gift for story telling with film know how and his business training, and began producing documentaries, first industrial and travel films, then Olympic films.

He found it both fun and rewarding, and might well have become the next Bud Greenspan, producing extraordinary videos about the drama of Olympic competition and the lonely struggles to reach the summit of Olympus. But Greg wanted to reach a wider audience, "more eyeballs," as he puts it.

But how? What to write?

He listed two essential criteria. It had to be something he knew well, and it had to be something that could not easily be stolen. In 1978, he came up with the idea for "Baywatch".

He first pitched the idea to Stu Irwin, who was working for media mogul, Grant Tinker. Irwin turned him down. It was the first of many such "no's" Greg would hear over the next ten years. But Greg was stubborn and, though discouraged, kept on pitching.

Finally, in 1987, he got a "yes!" Ironically, it was NBC's Irwin, the same guy who'd

been the first to turn him down, who finally was the one to say "yes."

Greg sold the rights to "Baywatch" to NBC and produced a successful pilot the next year. The show aired in 1989-90, making a major splash. Then, inexplicably, it was abruptly canceled by NBC. Deep sixed.

Undeterred, Greg saw opportunity where others would see disappointment. He bought the rights back from NBC and put the show into syndication.

The rest, as they say, is history. The series lasted another 11 years, the final two based in Hawaii. At the time, it was the longest running show on television, watched each week by an estimated one billion people in 140 countries on six continents and in 33 languages. Today, it can still be seen almost everywhere in rerun syndication.

How's that for "eyeballs"?

Bonann, who directed over 70 episodes of "Baywatch", including most of the action and rescue scenes, says the series was meant to chronicle the heroic efforts of the previously unsung LA County lifeguards. Thanks to his efforts, that is no longer the case.

Sometimes, reality and fiction seem to converge. One day, when Greg had arrived at the beach for a shoot, a terrified young boy ran up to him, pleading for his help. His brother, he blurted out, had been pulled out by the rip tide and was drowning. Greg stripped off his shirt and shoes, and stroked quickly, riding the rip current to where the boy had last been seen. He had to make three dives before he found the unconscious boy, who had been submerged on the murky bottom for over five minutes and wasn't breathing.

Greg quickly assessed the situation and realized there was no time to carry the boy back to the shore for CPR. So he immediately began performing mouth-to-mouth resuscitation while treading water. Greg saved the boy's life and was awarded the prestigious Medal of Valor for his heroic effort.

In addition, last year he and Tai (pronounced "tay") Collins, a former "Miss Virginia USA" and an accomplished television writer, sold a new show to a major network and are hard at work writing the pilot. It's called "Point Dune," and revolves around two central characters, a former Navy SEAL and a beach lifeguard, who take on troubled, at-risk teens and put them through a program designed to get them back on track. Of course there are life life-and-death situations in every episode. Collins describes the show as "empowering to teens."

Greg's proudest achievement, however, is the foundation he and Tai created in 1992 for homeless and at risk children. Greg underwrites all of the foundation's activities and

Tai serves as its unpaid Executive Director. "Everyone who works here is a volunteer," she explains.

Originally called "Camp Baywatch," it began as a program to give those children a chance to experience the beach (though they lived in L.A., most had never been to the beach) and an opportunity to learn how to swim and be safe at beaches and pools.

In 2000, it morphed into "A Chance for Children," with a much more ambitious agenda. It still has, as one focus, teaching inner city kids to swim. Tai explains, "Greg organizes everything connected with swimming. We might bring 35 kids at a time to Pepperdine University on Monday. None of them know how to swim and they're all terrified of the water. By Wednesday, they all can swim, the fear is gone and they're jumping off the high dive."

That's because Greg usually arranges one on one instruction, using Masters swimmers, other athletes, "Baywatch" cast members, lifeguards, fire fighters, police, military personnel and Olympians as instructors. Among the Olympians who have served are Gary Hall, Jr., John Naber and Summer Sanders.

The foundation's mission statement is "to inspire, educate and encourage youth to believe in themselves by providing them with exposure to worlds and opportunities that would otherwise not be available to them."

It certainly succeeds. Among the hundreds of activities it sponsors and has organized for L.A.'s inner city kids are:

College scholarships

Dance scholarships

Annual Christmas and Halloween parties

Providing school supplies

Trips to Washington, DC and Hawaii

Playing minor roles on episodes of "Baywatch"

Visits to a U.S. Coast Guard Air Station, Sea World, Disneyland, the zoo, Cultural trips to plays such as Shakespeare's "Romeo and Juliet", ballets such as "The Nutcracker", and trips to various ice shows, visits to amusement parks and whale watching outings

Sponsoring the Los Angeles Little League

Visits to various pro sports games including LA Kings hockey

Taking part in an NFL Super Bowl party with NFL players, combined with a

"Goals for "Life" program

Sponsoring a Computer Room for Chernow House, a shelter for homeless children
   "Kids Giving Back," on Nickelodeon with Shaquille O'Neal, Rosie O'Donnell,
   Whoopi Goldberg, Tim Allen, Tyra Banks, The Back Street Boys and other celebs.
And many other projects.

Greg and Tai's vision of educating and inspiring children expanded recently to include an international Learn to Swim program, dedicated to increasing awareness of the need to teach children around the world how to be safe in and around the water.

Greg thinks BIG, so it's not surprising that the goal of this program is nothing less than to remove drowning from the top of the Center for Disease Control's list of killers of children.

Greg was photographed August 1, 2005 in Malibu, California.
Profile contributed by Phil Whitten.

Rowdy Gaines

Growing up in the small town of Winter Haven, Florida, the water was almost as natural a habitat for Ambrose "Rowdy" Gaines IV as it was for the alligators, river otters, manatees and other aquatic creatures that call the state home.

Gaines grew up water skiing, swimming and horsing around in the 120 lakes that surrounded their town. "I learned to swim before I learned to walk," he says and swimming with alligators wasn't uncommon. "You could swim right alongside them then and they didn't do anything." says Gaines. "Now since their environment's more encroached on you hear about more attacks."

So even though he didn't start competing until the relatively ripe old age of 17, it's not that surprising that Gaines went on to become one of the most famous names in swimming. And he became legendary not only for his lightning speed, which lasted from the 50 all the way up to the 200 meters, but even more so for two dramatic psychological and physical comebacks and for his ongoing contributions to the sport.

Gaines tried practically all the other competitive sports offered in high school, basketball, baseball, football, golf and tennis, and claims he was a failure at them all. But when he got into the pool to compete for the first time, he knew he had found his element.

"The first day I started I fell in love with it. I said 'this is the sport,' I knew I had a passion for it. I didn't start with any grand illusions of being an Olympian, it was just something to do. I'd tried all the other sports and swimming was next in line."

Since he was relatively new to the sport, he improved rapidly as he refined his stroke technique and learned the ropes of the swimming world.

"I think I had a natural feel for the water as I grew up around it all my life, so I felt very comfortable as I grew older and stronger," he said. "My coach in high school was big motivation as well. He came from a football background and so he pushed me but never in a negative way."

Gaines was recruited to Auburn University in nearby Georgia by coach Eddie Reese. He excelled at Auburn, first under Reese and then under Richard Quick, known for producing fast swimmers and coaching with a strict, no-nonsense style. Gaines gained 22 All American honors and eight NCAA championships at Auburn, including individual golds in the 100 and 200 freestyle in both 1980 and 1981. "I grew from a boy to a man at Auburn," said Gaines, who majored in telecommunications there and planned to be a film director like his father, who has produced documentaries and TV ads including many for Ford and Dodge.

When the Olympic year 1980 rolled around, 21 year old Gaines was in top form, holding world records in the 100 and 200 meter free and favored to win five golds in Moscow. But that was the year that President Jimmy Carter decided to boycott the Games to oppose the Soviet Union's invasion of Afghanistan. So Gaines didn't get his chance at multiple Olympic gold.

"There were two reasons for the boycott, to get them to move the Games from Moscow or to get the Russians out of Afghanistan," says Gaines. "Neither one happened. If the boycott worked I would have been all for it, but it didn't."

He was terribly disappointed.

"The Olympics is like the Super Bowl for swimmers, except we can't go back the next year and try again," he notes.

When he graduated from Auburn the year after the boycott he also retired from swimming, like most swimmers did after college in those days, to get on with his life.

"After your senior year in college you moved on with your life," he said. "There wasn't any money involved in the sport so it was extremely difficult to swim six hours a day AND make a living. The boycott was a small part of it, I guess, but mostly it was the fact that I needed to move on to the real world."

But he couldn't stay away long. About eight months later he was back in training, having decided to shoot for the 1984 Olympics.

"After a summer of not doing much I came to the realization that I had to go back," he says. "I couldn't always be thinking what if."

His father helped convince him.

"He said, 'Look at yourself in the mirror. What will you think every time an Olympics rolls around? If you go for it and fail, at least you can say you went for it.'"

He started training again with Quick at Auburn, then moved with Quick when he became women's coach at the University of Texas in Austin, where Eddie Reese was the men's coach. Training there as a post graduate, "it was perfect because I had Richard and Eddie," he said. He didn't waste any time regaining his speed. In 1982 he broke his own world record in the 200 meter free and the following year at the Pan American Games in Caracas, Venezuela he won a gold in the 100 free.

At that time, before there was any money in swimming, making the Olympics at age

25 the way Gaines would was virtually unheard of. But Gaines did qualify for the team, coming in second in the 100 free at the 1984 Olympic Trials (and seventh in the 200 free).

At the Olympic Games in Los Angeles, he did not disappoint. He won gold in the 100 free, in an Olympic record just 0.45 of a second shy of his own world record in the event. He also scooped up gold medals in the 400 free and 400 medley relays. The 400 medley dream team of Gaines, Steve Lundquist, Pablo Morales and Rick Carey set a new world record.

"Going into the Olympics a lot of doubts crept up in my mind," he says. "But I knew when I got up on those blocks, I had three years more training than any of those other guys. My logic, dumb as it may sound, was that I deserved it because I had worked so much harder and longer. It was my time. Their time would be down the line."

Going into the final, Gaines was confident he was in good shape because he had qualified well in prelims without pulling out all the stops.

Quick told Gaines that if he backed off on his legs the first 50 and kept up with the field, he could win it in the second half.

"I backed off on my legs and I was still ahead of the field at the 50," he said.

Needless to say, he won. That capped a career that saw him set 11 world records and win 17 national championships.

"My dream was really to be an Olympian, to be able to say, 'I represented the U.S. at the Olympics,'" Gaines muses now. "When it was all over, I felt the journey would've been worth it even if I didn't win. The friendships, the traveling, being in shape... that's what you remember. I couldn't tell you what my best times were but I remember my friends and all the countries I visited."

Swimmers, coaches and fans around the country saw it as a monumental comeback, and praised the affable, lanky, exceedingly polite star for not letting the disappointment of the boycott get the best of him.

Little did Gaines and his supporters know that his biggest comeback was still ahead.

After the Olympics he moved to Las Vegas and took over a tiny team called Las Vegas Gold, bringing it from a team of about 30 to a national caliber program of over 300 swimmers. And in Las Vegas he met his wife to be Judy, the sister of a friend of his. But soon he was on the road so much for speaking engagements, clinics and other appearances that he worried the team was getting short shrift.

"I felt like they needed a full time coach," he said.

When he was in Japan for a swim clinic, he met the head of a Tokyo swim club who also ran the Oahu Club in Honolulu. An invitation for Gaines to serve as manager of the Oahu Club ensued.

"It was Hawaii!," he said. "I felt it would be a great experience for me and my family and it was."

The family lived there from 1989 to 1996, and Gaines also traveled to Japan several times to start Oahu Club programs there. During this time he also competed in Masters swimming himself, logging 23 Masters World Records.

In 1991, after he had just finished swimming in the chilly Long Island Sound as part of the Swim Across America fundraiser, he felt a tingling in his fingers and toes. Everyone naturally thought it was the cold or the exertion, but within 24 hours, Gaines was completely paralyzed. He was the victim of Guillain-Barre syndrome, a rare autoimmune neurological disorder that affects one in 100,000 Americans. Much remains a mystery about the illness, which is not contagious, and appears to be triggered by a respiratory or gastrointestinal infection or sometimes by surgery.

As terrifying as the experience is, patients usually do recover, so Gaines kept a positive attitude and figured he would make it. He spent six weeks in the hospital, and when he finally got to go home he had to relearn everything – walking, tying his shoes, holding a fork. Describing the experience now, he is markedly nonchalant about what must have been a grueling and traumatic period.

"My family was there for me, and I got an amazing outpouring of support," he said. "I got literally thousands of cards and letters. I probably still get a letter or e-mail every week from someone who has it, so I can send them words of encouragement."

He was fully paralyzed for two weeks and his recovery to normal levels of activity took about six months. Not surprisingly, his therapy included getting back in the water. Just a year after contracting the devastating illness he won two Masters World titles. Several years later, he surprised himself by making the cuts for the 1996 Olympic Trials in the 50 free, at age 37. He toyed with the idea of actually competing at Trials, but decided against it.

"I thought maybe I should go for fun, but I had to come back to reality a bit," he says. "I was only doing 3,000 or 4,000 (yards a day). I would have had to do a lot more than that. I had a family and other priorities by then. And NBC had offered me the job commentating."

Family became Gaines' top priority. He has four daughters – Emily, born in 1985, Madison in 1989, Savanna in 1994 and Isabelle in 1999. None of them is a swimmer. Madison says she would "rather eat dirt" than swim.

They don't really think much about his stellar swimming career, he says. "To them I'm just Dad."

After his recovery from Guillain-Barre, Gaines and his family moved back to Alabama for seven years, living in Auburn and then Birmingham.

Then in 2003 he started working for USA Swimming in Colorado Springs as the chief fundraising and alumni officer. The job includes doing outreach, starting new Learn to Swim programs and increasing minority participation in swimming, as well as organizing reunions of Olympic and National Team alumni. One of his suggestions to get more boys involved in swimming is to let them wear looser, more fashionable swimsuits at the recreational level instead of pushing them to wear skimpy racing suits.

Over the years he has also stayed involved in the sport and in promoting healthy lifestyles in various ways, including as a board member of Swim Across America, the Birmingham YMCA, the Speedo Advisory Board and several programs to involve inner city youth in swimming. He is also a spokesperson for the Children's Miracle Network and Endless Pools.

As well as having been a commentator for NBC at four Olympic Games, most recently in Athens in 2004, he has also done commentary for TNT, ESPN and CBS. He is scheduled to be commentator for NBC again during the 2008 Olympic Games in Beijing.

He has written for "Swimming World Magazine", "SWIM Magazine" and nbcolympics.com and was a contributing author on the book "Awaken The Olympian Within". He has also worked with Olympian John Moffett on instructional swimming videos.

In 2005 Gaines capped his long list of awards and honors with perhaps the ultimate – he was inducted into the U.S. Olympic Hall of Fame along with Olympic greats Evelyn Ashford, Peter Vidmar and Bob Beamon. Though he never wanted it to be the only thing he did, Gaines is glad that swimming still plays a major part in his life.

"All those things you learn in swimming carry over to the 'real' world," he says. "I'm hoping one day I'll be remembered for being a lot more than a swimmer. But if my tombstone says 'Rowdy Gaines – Swimmer' that will be okay too. It's a great sport."

Rowdy was photographed February 3, 2006 during the World Cup Series in Hempstead, New York.

Profile contributed by Kari Lydersen.

Biographies of Our Writers and Photographer/Editor

John Lohn is a sports journalist for the *Delaware County Daily Times*, located just outside of Philadelphia, Pennsylvania. He is a graduate of La Salle University. He handles collegiate, scholastic and Olympic sport coverage for the newspaper. He has been a regular contributor to *Swimming World Magazine* since 2000 and has served as the NewsMaster of SwimmingWorldMagazine.com since March of 2005.

Kari Lydersen is a staff writer for *The Washington Post* out of the Midwest bureau in Chicago. She graduated from Northwestern University with a degree in journalism in 1997. Along with writing for *The Washington Post*, she also freelances for *Swimming World Magazine* and various publications and is a youth journalism instructor and professor at Columbia College. She was a several time national team member in swimming and open water swimming and was a two time national champion in open water swimming (15K and 25K). She also swam for Northwestern University.

Jeremy Shweder is the former editor of *MetroSports New York* and *MetroSports Washington* magazine and has written hundreds of articles about endurance sports and about athletes of all shapes, sizes and speeds. He is a graduate of Swarthmore College, where he was a nationally ranked collegiate tennis player, and he also earned a graduate degree from Northwestern University School of Journalism. He currently lives in New York City and studies law.

Larry Thompson is the photographer and editor of the book. Although never a competitive swimmer, Larry has long been captivated by the purity of the sport and the character of those who make it great. Larry lives in Connecticut with his family. He can be reached at www.39AvenueRapp.com.

Bill Volckening is the United States Masters Swimming (USMS) National Publication Editor of *SWIMMER Magazine*. Before participating in the creation of *SWIMMER Magazine*, Volckening worked for five years as USMS Editor of *SWIM Magazine* with noted swimming journalist Phil Whitten. Volckening has written hundreds of articles for publications including *SWIM Magazine*, *Swimming World Magazine*, *Swimming Technique*, *Fitness Swimmer*, and *Triathlete* magazine. He also contributed to the book *It's Never Too Late* by Gail Kislevitz, and served for two years as a special web correspondent for USA Swimming. Volckening is the recipient of the 1999 USMS Newsletter of the Year Award, the 2000 and 2002 USMS Fitness Award, the 2001 Dorothy Donnelly USMS Service Award and the inaugural Phillip Whitten Pioneer Award for Journalism.

Phillip Whitten is an editor and Chief Media Officer for *Swimming World Magazine*. He is the author of *The Complete Book of Swimming* (Random House) and is the author or coauthor of eighteen books and over one hundred major articles on a wide variety of topics. He has lectured throughout the United States and several foreign countries on swimming and on fitness, health and the aging process. He has published pioneering studies on exercise, aging, sexuality and on the effects of exercise in forestalling biological and psychological aging. Dr. Whitten is acknowledged as one of the world's leading authorities on swimming. He is also a top Masters swimmer, having set several national and world records. An anthropologist and gerontologist, Whitten earned an interdisciplinary doctorate for Harvard University and has taught at Harvard University, Bentley College, and Endicott College.

To Learn More About Our Swimmers and Their Organizations of Interest

Melanie Benn	www.challengedathletes.org
Greg Bonnan	www.achanceforchildren.org
George Brunstad	www.centerofhope-hati.org
Lynne Cox	www.lynnecox.org
Maritza Correia	www.pmgsports.com
Dave Denniston	www.davedenniston.com
Rowdy Gaines	www.makeasplash.org
Dawn Blue Gerken	www.lupus.org
Jeff Keith	www.ctchallenge.org
Terry Laughlin	www.totalimmersion.net
Marcella MacDonald	www.channelswimming.com
Mike Nyeholt	www.swimwithmike.org
Chris Swain	www.swimforcleanwater.com
Noah White	www.usna.edu
David Yudovin	www.davidyodovinchannelswimmer.com

To Learn More About

The National Swimming Pool Foundation

The National Swimming Pool Foundation® (NSPF®) is a 42 year old non-profit 501(c)(3) organization dedicated to improving public health worldwide by attracting more people to safer aquatic environments. NSPF® is committed to improving public health by encouraging healthier living through aquatic education and research. The foundation is the leading educator for pool and spa professionals who service and operate public and private pools and spas and for public health officials who are responsible for pool safety. NSPF® works towards its mission with educational products like the Certified Pool-Spa Operator® (CPO®) training, Certified Pool-Spa Inspector™ (CPI™) training, the Pool Math™ Workbook, the Aquatic Safety Compendium™, eProAcademy™ online training center and the World Aquatic Health™ Conference. Proceeds from our educational products support the foundation and are reinvested into research grants, fellowships, new educational programs, scientific conferences and a scholarly journal. The NSPF® funds grants to help reduce risk at aquatic facilities. The foundation also is the largest funding source for grants to study aquatic health benefits in swimming pools and hot tubs.

To learn more about the NSPF® contact Thomas M. Lachocki, Ph.D., CEO at 719-540-9119 or email to media@nspf.org or visit www.nspf.org and www.eProAcademy.org.